Embedded Autonomy

Kevin Muldoon-Smith
Mark Sandford • Greg Stride
Andrew Walker

Embedded Autonomy

Financing a Resilient Local Government Effectively

palgrave
macmillan

Kevin Muldoon-Smith
Northumbria University
Newcastle, UK

Mark Sandford
University of Bristol
Bristol, UK

Greg Stride
Local Democracy Research Centre
Local Government Information Unit
London, UK

Andrew Walker
Local Democracy Research Centre
Local Government Information Unit
London, UK

ISBN 978-981-97-9029-6 ISBN 978-981-97-9030-2 (eBook)
https://doi.org/10.1007/978-981-97-9030-2

This Palgrave Macmillan imprint is published by the registered company Springer Nature Singapore Pte Ltd.
The registered company address is: 152 Beach Road, #21-01/04 Gateway East, Singapore 189721, Singapore

Acknowledgements

Over the last ten years, the indications that there has been a major sustained failure to properly fund local services in England have grown in profile. The central motivation in this book is to consider, in that context, how England could fund its local government differently. How can the continual hand to mouth existence of local authorities, and those that work to support them, be improved? While there has been plenty of rhetoric and policy initiative around devolution of power to local authorities in recent decades, continuing recently with the English Devolution Bill, there has been far less attention paid to how any of these endeavours will be practically delivered and, most importantly, funded. Consequently, this book tries to give a more balanced view of the function and funding of local government and, in doing so, attempts to open a wider conversation around what local government is actually for in England in the absence of any codified constitution, and to provide a more positive account of local government delivery.

Not only does local government need a new financial programme—it also needs a progressive intellectual basis upon which a new programme can sit. In this book, we utilise system-based thinking to understand local government finance as a holistic entity and forward *embedded autonomy* as a new way of framing and perhaps uniting the competing aims from central and local government for their own autonomy. Embedded autonomy attempts to harness a perception-based tightrope where too much surrender to local autonomy harms wider society and too much constraint on local autonomy prevents local government from operating efficiently. Currently debate and traditional practice operates at the extremes of this tightrope, more so the centralising tendency. We propose a system that balances both.

This book is the initial output of a research project led by Kevin Muldoon-Smith at Northumbria University, in partnership with Mark Sandford at Bristol University and the Local Government Information Unit (LGIU), which is seeking to understand how local government finance works internationally, with a view to informing how practice and reform can be instigated in England. The initial case study locations, Germany, Italy, and Japan, have offered rich insights for how improvements can be made in England. These locations have also been useful in highlighting that England is not alone in struggling with local authority insolvency and wider questions of how to fund public services. However, these locations do things differently and our conclusions indicate that they do many things better.

This international focus also opens a two-way interaction, between England and international best practice, where each can learn from the other. This process has helped to communicate the practice and experiences of local government to an international audience. However, an additional motivation in the research was to underline the role local government finance plays in questions of governance, territorial development, economic growth and, at its root, the life chances of citizens in any given location. The intention is that drawing the attention of a multidisciplinary audience to local government finance will help to answer the underlying question in this book—what if English local government was funded differently?

In carrying out this research, and writing this book, there has been considerable use made of existing government and constitutional documentation, especially as it relates to the structure and regulation of local government finance systems. Throughout the project there has also been continual support from civil servants, council officers, local councillors, and politicians who have all been vital in understanding the technical detail and esotericism of local government finance sources, and the local democratic interaction with an often-opaque system of working. Thanks go to the research assistants who have helped support this project throughout the project journey: Cameron Forbes, Sara Lilley, and Yoshio Shimbo. Each played a significant role in developing the initial reporting in each location and particularly translating documentation from the different international contexts. Special thanks go to Jonathan Pearson who had a hand in the analysis of all three case study locations.

Thanks are extended to those experts who have helped direct our enquiry in each country. Stuart Hoggan and Mike Woods have provided invaluable insights into the historical operation of the local government finance system in England, helping to point out the reality and challenges of central government efforts to deliver change, both from a central and local government perspective. Andrew Stevens has been a valuable source of insight into the workings of the Japanese local government finance system, signposting us to additional contacts and information sources. Francesco Porcelli has been a continual point of reference in the Italian local government finance system, highlighting that some of England's often derided previous practice have been taken forward as underlying parts of successful local government systems overseas. Thanks are also due to Peter Eckersley, Rene Geissler, and Steffen Zabler, all of whom improved the underlying understanding of the German system of local government finance. All of these colleagues helped to avoid only taking on board the elements of these international case studies that appeared to support critique of the English system—highlighting how the challenges in each country make the case for reform in England far stronger.

Thanks also go to all of those involved in the book's production, Marion Duvall and Connie Li at Palgrave for the understanding and direction through the publishing process, the anonymous reviews at proposal and final submission, and all of those who have provided comments on either sub-section, chapters, or the full manuscript. In terms of the refinement of the proposals in this book, thanks go to participants at various LGIU-led sessions with local councillors, special interest groups, and various government departments who have all provided comments and helped to road test and develop the central arguments.

While all attempts have been made to capture the technical detail in each country, all errors are the authors' own.

Kevin Muldoon-Smith
Mark Sandford
Greg Stride
Andrew Walker

Contents

List of Figures

List of Tables

1

Introduction

This book is engaged with the financial uncertainty currently facing the local government sector in England. It seeks to explain the reasons why this situation has arisen and the implications for public service delivery in the coming years. It then systematically examines examples of international best practice to understand how the local government finance system in England could be improved. It then presents a set of proposals for reform to the English local government finance system that encapsulates the principles of what the authors call *embedded autonomy*. It argues that local government in England cannot stand on its own two feet without a resilient[1] and well-funded local government finance system based on cooperation, fairness, and scrutiny.

England's councils are in serious financial trouble. Six, including Birmingham, Nottingham, and Croydon, have issued "section 114 notices", indicating an undeliverable budget, since 2020.[2] A cross-party

[1] Financial resilience in this book is taken to mean enough meaningful funding to fairly fund the local government finance system in good time and certainty alongside transparent and rigorous negotiation, monitoring, and scrutiny procedures.

[2] Issuing a section 114 notice is often described as 'bankruptcy' in media coverage. This is not correct as English local authorities cannot go bankrupt. A section 114 notice is issued by a chief finance officer (section 151 officer) if they have reason to believe their authority is about to incur

K. Muldoon-Smith et al., *Embedded Autonomy*,
https://doi.org/10.1007/978-981-97-9030-2_1

report published by the Levelling up, Housing and Communities Select Committee in the House of Commons, at the beginning of 2024, stated that government must plug a £4 billion funding gap to have any chance of financial resilience in the short to medium term (2024), while later in the year the Local Government Association placed this figure at £6.2 billion (2024). Not since the poll tax riots in the early 1990s have issues of local government finance and taxation figured so prominently in public debate.

Various organisations have begun to take note of this situation and approach solutions from several perspectives, in relation to place-based budgeting (Denham & Studdert, 2024), devolution (Institute for Government, 2023), liberating public services (Demos, 2024), streamlining of the grants system (Centre for Cities, 2023), and the overall reform of the local government finance system (Local Government Information Unit, 2024). This echoes intermittent calls for reform in the 2000s and 2010s (Travers & Esposito, 2004) and continual advice from the Institute for Fiscal Studies (2024) and Charted Institute for Public Finance and Accountancy (CIPFA) during the same period (2019) in relation to the financial resilience of local government finance.

While six section 114 notices represent a small fraction of the 317 local authorities in England, it can be argued that the entire local government finance system in England is teetering. This situation has only been sharpened by the impact of the Covid-19 pandemic, inflation, energy costs, economic stagnation, and in-built uncertainty in the current method of allocating funding from central government. Now, each year, local authorities must continually make challenging decisions in relation to what not to fund, rather than meaningfully considering how best to represent local citizens and how to develop their local areas.

Demonstrating the system-wide struggles in local government, in March 2024, 19 local authorities were granted exceptional financial support for the 2024–2025 financial year. This comprised permission for local authorities to use capital receipts or borrowing to cover revenue costs in their budgets, up to a total value of £1.5bn in the 2024–2025

---

unlawful expenditure, including if they will not be able to balance their budget in the financial year. A section 114 notice indicates severe financial difficulties that must be resolved at speed.

financial year. While this flexibility has helped fend off bankruptcy in the short term, it also highlights the unusual practices that are being utilised by the local government sector to survive. The mixing of capital finance with that of revenue is a highly unusual accountancy procedure (Webb, 2024), and ties local authorities to debt liability in the medium to long term. Reminiscent of the banking system collapse in 2008, some local authorities are literally borrowing across the medium to long term to fill immediate funding shortages. The split between revenue and capital budgets was previously a key principle that underpinned prudence, budgetary stewardship and medium-term financial sustainability.

This situation follows a period of sustained austerity and financial retrenchment in the local government sector—the total spending power of local government has declined significantly since 2010 (Muldoon-Smith & Sandford, 2021). There has almost been a path-dependent assumption in recent years that demands for austerity require the government to pursue reductions in local government spending without limits. But this assumption overlooks the role of local government in delivering on political goals that are often shared with central government: pared-back funding has eroded the ability of local government to act and, in doing so, damaged the capacity of central government to drive change.

English local government now faces existential funding questions. The local government finance situation should be a concern for all political parties irrespective of their time in power or political leaning. It might be tempting for a new reforming government to regard local authority financial failures as a minor inconvenience that can be tolerated when there are bigger fish to fry. However, as Will Hutton (2024) recently argued in the *Observer*, England is discovering that the local is political: that society begins with good access to social care and regular bin collections. Councils are critical delivery partners for any UK government. If financial difficulties hobble their capacity to act, the government loses time and capacity too. Local government finance is notoriously technically complex, unrewarding, and politically arduous: but the situation in England, coupled with the ambitions of the government elected in 2024, means that not tackling local government finance's predicament is now extraordinarily risky.

There has been a great deal of attention given in recent years to big ticket national and foreign policy items—Brexit, immigration, war. In contrast, almost through a process of deliberate myopia, the economic, social, and community role of local government has been largely overlooked. Scholarly and media attention has focused on devolution of power to novel sub-national governance arrangements, many featuring metro mayors.[3] This book argues that there needs to be a reset and change in mindset in relation to local government finance. While Chancellor Rachel Reeves has placed emphasis on stringent fiscal rules and even reshaping markets to form a 'securonomics' at the national scale, and growth at the regional scale, there needs to be the same emphasis on financial resilience at the local scale. A major mission of any government should be stability of local government finances. Recognising that the financial resilience of local government is a systemic part of the regional and national economy is the starting point for any reform of local government finance systems, to restore certainty and discretion and encourage new ideas around autonomy and resilience.

This is the mission of this book. We build up a body of evidence through each chapter that makes clear that local government finance reform should be based on co-dependent principles of embedded autonomy and financial system-based resilience. The principle of embedded autonomy draws, in part, on the work of Peter Evans (1995) who applied the concept of embedded autonomy to the developmental state, to define a government process that supported industrial development, without becoming predatory. The 'embedded' component recognises that the state and society are entwined, while 'autonomy' recognises that businesses need the right incentives to set goals and develop within a system of continuous renegotiation.[4] It contrasts with the model of bidding and 'earned autonomy' (Jones & Stewart, 2002) favoured in recent decades and rigid conceptualisations of resilience.[5]

---

[3] The local elections in May 2024 were arguably the largest devolved election in the history of England. Eleven metro-mayors now govern half of the electorate in England (12 if London is included). Yet it is currently unclear how far the existing cohort of metro-mayors can align their multi-million-pound funding streams to buttress local authority services and structures.

[4] Evans's work has been taken forward since. E.g., Jacobs (2003) has used the concept to critique metropolitan development in North America, Clark and Rosales (2022) have investigated the Latin American Pink Tide, and Styhre (2019) has used it to consider the institutional history of the firm.

[5] In arguing for embedded autonomy and resilience we do not refute the role of the state in local government finance. Rather, we try to suggest how both could work harmoniously.

Focus of the Book

> Councils have faced a prolonged war of attrition from above. Over the last decade or so, councils have faced severe financial pressures resulting from tight limits imposed from above, increased demands from below, and the difficulties of raising sufficient local tax revenue. (Cochrane, 1993, p. 2)

This quote from Cochrane (1993) could easily describe the circumstances of local government today. The challenges that the sector currently faces are not new. The English local government finance system has faced uncertainties and pressures for decades. Yet the current reasons for this are often unclear and the potential future trajectories of local government finance are equally contested (Hawksbee, 2022; Mudie et al., 2023). The aim of the book is to develop a distinctive approach to understanding the local government finance system, as a complex adaptive system, and to point towards potential future directions for local government financing. This amounts to challenging the assumption that it is sustainable to fund local government out of the current financial model.

Cochrane's seminal *Whatever Happened to Local Government?* remains as relevant today as it was on the day it was published in 1993. However, the vast majority of scholarly contributions to local government finance learning have coalesced around the critical financialisation literature in recent years—particularly the impact of capital markets on local authority decision making and power relations. Perhaps first gaining real prominence with Rachel Weber in 2010 with her research into tax increment financing in Chicago, several authors have taken the study of financialisation forward: Fields (2018) in relation to automated landlords, Peck and Whiteside (2016) in relation to local authority bankruptcy in Detroit, and latterly Beswick and Penny (2018) in relation to municipal financialisation, Penny (2022) in relation to local housing companies as revenue generating machines, and Pike (2023) in relation to local authority investment and statecraft. There is now a considerable international literature around financialisation, particularly examining the interaction of capital markets, the state in its various guises, land and property development, and physical assets (see Ward et al., 2024 for a summary of future research directions in financialisation and Hasenberger 2024 for an account of financialisation and its relation with local government).

However, the findings and recommendations in this book are foregrounded by a belief that the exponential growth in financialisation literature has clouded the underlying role of local government or municipal finance structures in the provision of services, governance, and local place making. In the UK, financialisation plays a relatively minor role in local government finance. Opportunities for the influence of financialisation on local government funding are heavily contingent on structures of governance in any given state and the underlying economic conditions in each location—often the *right* conditions are rare and restricted to a minority of premium locations (Muldoon-Smith & Greenhalgh, 2015). The volume of publications can mean that financialisation threatens to take on an outsized role in the local government financial debate, in the absence of any alternative analysis of the local government finance system in England.

Mundane questions of the funding of local authorities—overwhelmingly the greatest concern for local authority solvency in terms of quantum of money and impact on local areas—have received less attention. Studies do exist of the stresses caused by funding reductions (e.g., Gray & Barford, 2018; Hastings et al., 2015), but they focus on critiquing central decision-making and do not attempt to explore alternative models of financing.

This book, therefore, focuses on the financial pressures faced by local government in England during recent decades and asks a simple question: How could local government be funded differently? This focus, and central question, enables us to ask the following core research questions:

1. How does the local government finance system currently work in England?
2. To what extent do existing and proposed sources of income address the solvency challenge in English local government?
3. What can international systems of local government finance tell us about potential options for reform in the English local government finance system?

4. How can transition into more progressive modes of local government financial working take place?

The authors examine these questions for several reasons. First, sharp reductions in central government grant funding in England since 2010 (Gray & Barford, 2018) have driven significant concerns over the current and future solvency of English local authorities and the asymmetric nature of austerity—local authorities have not been able to replace these transfer grants with equivalent sums of locally generated income. Second, these concerns have, in turn, generated advocacy and proposals for increased fiscal decentralisation in parallel to arguments in favour of devolution, embedded in a long-term disquiet at British centralism. Third, this latter debate, so far, has been stunted. UK governments have avoided grasping the nettle of considering the structure of local government funding since the replacement of the Community Charge by council tax in the early 1990s, preferring no or incremental change. But equally, calls from the sector for fiscal devolution (LGA, 2022; Copus et al., 2017) have often disregarded the political ramifications of devolving revenue-raising powers, risking the appearance of demands for cash from one interest group among many. The consequence is that while literature, lobbying, and policy change have grown significantly in relation to devolution, examination of the finance system that underpins both local authorities and metro-mayors has been limited and superficial. Taking this argument to its logical conclusion, greater fiscal devolution could easily exacerbate the problem of uneven service provision because poorer areas are less well-placed to generate their own revenue.

Impact and Significance

The originality in this book is found in its alternative perspective of local government finance—encapsulated in the underlying system-based perspective and the new conceptual formulation *embedded autonomy*. Originality is also found in the analysis of international case studies to inform potential change in England and its consequent focus on reform in England. The central arguments and findings in the book, while related to England, also have broader application. England has long been seen as a laboratory for new forms and techniques of policy and governance (Pike et al., 2019). All countries have unique central–local contexts and administrative procedures for funding their public services. However, the initial findings and wider discussion in this book provide a factual source for policymakers (and those that provide scrutiny) to evaluate and propose new initiatives for funding local government. For professionals struggling with the day-to-day management of local government funding, the book provides an overview of the constraints and challenges of rewiring the funding of statutory obligations. The findings will serve to assist international efforts to stabilise and strengthen systems of local government, which can fall prey to abstract demands for 'more powers' with little underpinning evidence. Examining the nature, agency, and techniques of local government funding systems—and the path dependencies they can unwittingly introduce—sheds a new light on international academic debates surrounding (1) how territories are funded, remain solvent, and develop over time; and (2) how this concern interfaces with wider geographies of development and political imperatives toward equalisation between territories.

The Underlying Arguments and Arrangement of the Book

This book argues that analyses of the financial challenges faced by England's local authorities typically focus on single elements of the finance system. For example, considerations of local authority decision-making take place without consideration of the sector's relationship with central government; or demands for local government autonomy omit any consideration of equalisation[6] between locations. While practitioners and academics often refer to the local government finance 'system', they rarely adopt a system-based analysis. The result is a set of arguments that

[6] Traditionally equalisation can take two forms: (1) vertical equalisation refers to the distribution of income from the state while (2) horizontal equalisation refers to the distribution of income between local areas, based on a ratio of relative local need and economic circumstance.

either favour a sharp extension of local financial autonomy or defaulting to the converse situation of centralised control—ignoring the co-dependent role each tier of government plays in contemporary local government finance systems. The aim of this book is to counter this situation by placing local government finance in a wider *complex system perspective*. In other words, local government finance challenges, practices, and options for reform can only be understood in the context of the functions of local authorities; capital finance and its regulation; audit and budgeting practice; funding redistribution and socioeconomic variations; and the often-uneven culture of central-local relations.

This system is made up of multiple agents and networks: for example, local government officers, civil servants, politicians, think tanks, audit authorities, lenders, and financiers who all have their own legal obligations, objectives, and decision-making frameworks. All of these elements interact with each other over time to form a whole that is more than the sum of its individual agents' objectives. It is this complex system of actors, regulations, and institutions that enables and constrains local government finance. Calls for additional funding or tax-raising powers, and more recent unorthodox borrowing practices, often emerge from, and are constrained by, this broader and connected context. However, the interactions between the different elements of the system are often disregarded, resulting in a partial understanding or misrepresentation of the local government finance challenge. We argue that it is not possible to comprehend local government by focusing on one component, authority, or agent. A holistic system-based approach is necessary.

The following chapter, Chap. 2, sets out this system-based perspective and centres it in current local government research paradigms. The chapter also mobilises critical juncture literature to argue that the mid-2020s provide an opportune moment to consider and influence reform of the local government finance system in England. We concede that we have only looked at three international locations—three out of countless local government finance systems in the world. However, the aim of the book is not to provide an exhaustive account of international practices. Rather the aim is to look at examples of international best practice, particularly locations that have gone through transition, reform, and/or stand out as examples of progressive and resilient local government finance systems.

Chapter 3 helps to foreground this analysis by outlining the operation of local government finance in England, and how its system-based features frame and constrain local government finance practitioner behaviour. The chapter argues that underlying systems of finance are a unique lens for understanding the operation and role of local government, offering a critical interpretation of recent local government finance reform in England and the impact this has on local government, place, and territorial development. In particular, in the English context, it argues that most sources of funding—both current and novel—provide both peripheral and geographically uneven quantities of revenue, and the link to local economic development is at best fuzzy. Chapter 3 then highlights the relatively peripheral role assumed by methods of financialisation within English local government. The effects are felt principally through influence on decision-making around infrastructure, in a minority of premium locations. The effects are muted where underlying land values are low and substantial profits are not available to investors. Chapter 3 concludes by setting out the underlying methodology for the empirical analysis in this book.

Chapter 4 takes the system interpretation further, offering a system-based analysis that outlines the challenges faced by local government finance in England, and the constraining influence of system features on the financial practices in local government. This chapter provides the foregrounding for the international analysis in the following chapters, and the suggestions for reform in Chap. 8. Chapters 5, 6, and 7 summarise an investigation into the operations of local government finance in international locations, namely, Germany, Italy, and Japan.

These international systems are analysed for two underlying reasons: (1) to understand how alternative financing arrangements are embedded and operate in alternative local government systems, and (2) to highlight the alternative perspectives of local government that are embodied in those systems, and how these contrast with prevalent assumptions and practices in England. Chapter 8 is then concerned with taking the outcomes of this research forward to suggest potential reforms in England in the short, medium, and long term. Chapter 9 summarises and elaborates on the central arguments in the book and proposals for reform. In particular, it focuses on embedded autonomy as a progressive framework for local government finance and more meaningful central-local relations.

At the core of our argument is the contention that England should not think of itself as an outlier in regard to local government finance. Rather, there is considerable opportunity to look overseas and note the experience of other local government finance systems as they have had to chart the evolutionary pains of system transition and new modes of working in recent years.

References

Beswick, J., & Penny, J. (2018). Demolishing the present to sell off the future? The emergence of 'financialized municipal entrepreneurialism' in London. *International Journal of Urban and Regional Research, 42*(4), 612–632. https://doi.org/10.1111/1468-2427.12612

Centre for Cities. (2023, June 8). *Potluck: What government needs to do to streamline local government funding.* Centre for Cities Briefing.

Chartered Institute for Public Finance and Accountancy. (2019). *An introductory guide to local government finance.* CIPFA.

Clark, P., & Rosales, A. (2022). Broadened embedded autonomy and Latin America's pink tide: Towards the neo-developmental state. *Globalizations, 20*(1), 20–37. https://doi.org/10.1080/14747731.2022.2032986

Cochrane, A. (1993). *What ever happened to local government?* Open University Press.

Copus, C., Robert's, M., & Wall, R. (2017). *Local government in England: Centralisation, autonomy and control.* Palgrave Macmillan.

Demos. (2024). *Liberated public services: A new vision for citizens, professionals and policy makers.* Demos.

Denham, J., & Studdert, J. (2024). *Place-based public service budgets: Making public money work better for communities.* New Local.

Evans, P. (1995). *Embedded autonomy: States and industrial transformation.* Princeton University Press.

Fields, D. (2018). Constructing a new asset class: Property-led financial accumulation after the crisis. *Economic Geography, 94*(2), 118–140. https://doi.org/10.1080/00130095.2017.1397492

Gray, M., & Barford, A. (2018). The depths of the cuts: The uneven geography of local government austerity. *Cambridge Journal of Regions, Economy and Society, 11*(3), 541–563. https://doi.org/10.1093/cjres/rsy019

Hasenberger, H. (2024). What is local government financialisation? Four empirical channels to clarify the roles of local government. *Urban Studies, 61*(11), 2039–2059. https://doi.org/10.1177/00420980231222133

Hastings, A., Bailey, N., & Gannon., K. Besemer., & G. Bramley. (2015). Coping with the cuts? The Management of the Worst Financial Settlement in living memory. *Local Government Studies, 41*(4), 601–621. https://doi.org/10.1080/03003930.2015.1036987

Hawksbee, A. (2022). *Give Back control: Realising the potential of England's mayors*. UK Onward.

Hutton, W. (2024, February 4). *The Tories starved councils, thinking no one cared. Now they're bust—And we care very much*. The Observer.

Institute for Fiscal Studies. (2024). *How have English councils' funding and spending changed? 2010 to 2024*. IFS.

Institute for Government. (2023). *How can devolution deliver regional growth in England*. Institute for Government.

Jacobs, A. J. (2003). Embedded autonomy and uneven metropolitan development: A comparison of the Detroit and Nagoya auto regions, 1969-2000. *Urban Studies, 40*(2), 335–360. https://doi.org/10.1080/00420980220080301

Jones, G., & Stewart, J. (2002). Central-local relations since the Layfield report. *Local Government Studies, 28*(3), 7–28. https://doi.org/10.1080/714004155

Local Government Association. (2022). *Reforming revenues: Options for the future financing of local government*. LGA.

Local Government Association. (2024). *Local government white paper*. LGA.

Local Government Information Unit. (2024). *The state of local government finance*. LGIU.

Mudie, R., Singh, T., Fogden, R., Franklin, B., & Geddis, P. (2023). *Funding fair growth: How to transform the UK economy*. Centre for Progressive Policy.

Muldoon-Smith, K., & Greenhalgh, P. (2015). Passing the buck without the bucks: Some reflections on fiscal decentralisation and the business rate retention scheme in England. *Local Economy, 30*(6), 609–626. https://doi.org/10.1177/0269094215599724

Muldoon-Smith, K., & Sandford, M. (2021). Grasping the nettle: The central–local constraints on local government funding in England. *Territory, Politics, Governance, 1-18*. https://doi.org/10.1080/21622671.2021.1924249

Peck, J., & Whiteside, H. (2016). Financializing Detroit. *Economic Geography, 92*(3), 235–268. https://doi.org/10.1080/00130095.2015.1116369

Penny, J. (2022). Revenue generating machines? London's local housing companies and the emergence of the local state rentierism. *Antipode, 54*(2), 545–566. https://doi.org/10.1111/anti.12774

Pike, A. (2023). *Financialization and local statecraft*. Oxford University Press—United Kingdom.

Pike, A., O'Brien, P., Strickland, T., & Tomaney, J. (2019). Financialising city statecraft and infrastructure; book symposium. *Environment and Planning A, 52*(4), 790–813. https://doi.org/10.1177/0308518X19889058

Styhre, A. (2019). *The institutional theory of the firm: Embedded autonomy*. Routledge.

Travers, T., & Esposito, L. (2004). *Nothing to lose but your chains: Reforming the English local government finance system*. Policy Exchange.

Ward, W., Brill, F., Deruytter, L., & Pike, A. (2024). Local state financialisation: Future research directions for an emergent conjuncture. *Finance and Space, 1*(1), 318–339. https://doi.org/10.1080/2833115X.2024.2380004

Webb, C. (2024. March 11). *Exceptional financial support is general election holding strategy*. Local Government Chronicle.

2

Time for System Thinking: A System-wide Perspective of Local Government Finance

In recent years, there has been considerable tension in England between the push for a fluid form of local government built upon local discretion, accountability, decentralisation, and autonomy and the more traditional imperative from the centre for a more static approach that prioritises central financial assurance and policy and outcome certainty. The central argument in this book is that local government financial autonomy and resilience are two sides of the same coin, and one cannot exist without the other—this is the essence of *embedded autonomy*. All too often each aspect is seen in opposition, with autonomy seen as a threat to the overall resilience of the local government finance system and resilience, bolstered by redistribution and transfer grant systems, seen as a barrier to autonomous working. Instead, we argue that local discretion and autonomy underpins resilience, enabling planning for, and reaction to, change. Local autonomy, discretion, and resilience can only be fostered by a wider system-based perspective of local government equalisation and budget certainty.

Local government cannot fulfil a role as a provider of services or as a place leader without a need-based and redistributive local government finance system. This has been implicit in most of the history of local government finance in the UK (Foster et al., 1980; Keith-Lucas & Richards,

K. Muldoon-Smith et al., *Embedded Autonomy*,
https://doi.org/10.1007/978-981-97-9030-2_2

1978) and indeed elsewhere. Without such a system, only those locations with an element of self-sufficiency based on buoyant income sources will thrive. This questions some of the arguments around local self-sufficiency and autonomy that have almost become an article of faith in recent years. Engaging in place-based activity is only an option for all authorities if they are connected into a system of local-state interaction. In other words, local government autonomy is located within, and supported by, continual system-based intergovernmental cooperation and interstate relations. While this contention may set the authors as atheists among believers in unfettered local autonomy, we believe more progressive place-based governance cannot work without an embedded connection with inter-territorial systems of local government finance. Aspirations towards "self-sufficient local government" (the title of a 2016 Government white paper) risk inadvertently creating disconnected entities that have as little capacity to govern their local places as under the current centralised arrangement.

New analytical frameworks and practical tools are needed to understand this permanent tension and complex interconnection between autonomy and resilience. To this end, we argue that the local government finance system should be considered and managed as part of a complex adaptive system, rather than a simplified system of control. Examples of complex adaptive systems include the stock market, climate, the brain, and business organisations (Preiser, 2018). The local government finance *system* is also a complex adaptive system that blends and conflicts consideration of local autonomy and financial resilience.

To explore this situation, intentionally, the book does not attempt to delve into the minutiae of local government finances, nor does it attempt to deliver statistical analysis[1] of the myriad financial details in each country. Moreover, while concentrating on local government finance, it does not present its arguments only through the prism of the local state or formulations of place. This is because the authors believe debates concerning local government financial autonomy and resilience can often get bogged down in esotericisms of process and accountancy—drowned out

[1] See the Institute for Fiscal Studies (2024) for technical analysis of many of the local government finance characteristics that we discuss.

in surface level statistical accounts of performance or restricted by local interpretations of governance and accountability. These perspectives can end up masking or ignoring how the local government finance system actually works—the contradictions, the local (and national) frustrations, and the behavioural and territorial consequence of everyday practice.

This is not to detract from more formal and technical appreciations of local government finance, nor place-based arguments for autonomy and resilience—each are a fundamental part of the foundation of any local government finance system. Rather, we are attempting to open a wider conversation and perspective about the functioning of the overall local government finance system. We hope this will help drive a debate around how the local government finance system in England can transition into a more resilient mode of autonomy and local representation under conditions of uncertainty and continual financial pressure.

Uncertainty is now a fundamental part of the make-up of any local government system in an increasingly dynamic world of competing aims, objectives, and external influences. It is now clear that local government operates in a context of continual volatility and pressure, managing the fallout from pandemic events, inflation, climate adaptation, the dynamic and variegated nature of place-based objectives, and the increasing pressure on protected health, social care, and education services. The complex system perspective offers a framework for understanding how a resilient local government finance system can be enabled in a context of multiple challenges facing local government in England—navigating the tension between local discretion and national control and certainty. This is achieved by recognising the complex interactions involved in local government finance, between different stakeholders and scales of government.

The Complexity Perspective

The complexity perspective considers the world to be dynamic, changing, and inherently uncertain, and is underpinned by the assertion that you cannot understand complex systems by looking at their individual parts or prioritising one agent or factor. In this sense, complexity in the local government finance system points away from a system with minimised regulation, scrutiny, and oversight: instead, it demands a more nuanced local government finance system that acknowledges and seeks to enable local government discretion. Adopting this perspective offers an insight into how different scales of local government can coexist successfully—and which approaches to funding optimise that coexistence.

The complex system perspective has taken root in several domains: urban planning (Zellner & Campbell, 2015; Sengupta et al., 2016; Skrimizea et al., 2018) natural resource management (Arnold, 2010; Kato & Ahern, 2008; van Buuren et al., 2013), adaptive management (Arnold, 2010; Patterson et al., 2008; Westley, 2002), adaptive policy making (Haasnoot et al., 2013), and adaptive governance (Dietz et al., 2003), where the position has gained some traction. However, the position is less prevalent in the domain of local government finance and the wider domain of local government studies—Klijn (2008), Bovaird (2008), and Rhodes and MacKechnie (2003) are notable exceptions with research into public administration and best value, Geyer and Rihani (2010) and Geyer and Cairney (2015) into public policy development, Lowe et al. (2021) into human learning systems and French et al. (2023) into public outcomes. Demos (2024) have recently referred to complexity at the local scale when considering the liberalisation of public services. Overall, however, it remains the case that the sector, and scholarly studies of the sector, rarely consider local government finance as a complex system. It remains the case that while we often refer to the *local government finance system* in debate, we seldom ever analyse it as a system or consider reforms or policy interventions from a system perspective.

The intention therefore is to extend system considerations into the domain of local government finance. The complex system approach opens the possibility of moving beyond binary positions of local discretion and national certainty, recognising that if local government finance and the wider system of local government are to adapt to more dynamic socio-economic conditions they need to acknowledge the balance and tension between these two imperatives. For example, in the English case, many individual aspects of the local government finance system have been subject to relatively minor procedural reforms that in turn impact and restrict other elements of the system, often disproportionately or in unforeseen ways. It therefore follows that more considerable changes to individual features in that system—such as a new tax-raising power or a changed approach to redistribution—could have considerable knock-on effects elsewhere within the system. Witness the pains in 2013 when the UK government introduced 50% business rate retention in parallel with unreconciled business rate revaluations; or the growth in commercial property investments by some authorities in the late 2010s, as an ostensibly open route to additional revenue funds when most alternative routes had become inadequate or unavailable.

As such, we argue that the aim of local government finance, as it relates to wider local government practice and studies, should not be to reduce uncertainty, nor to control complexity, but to "understand and harness" these factors and develop a local government finance system that "co-adapts" and "co-evolves" (Skrimizea et al., 2018, p. 131) alongside dynamic changes in the external environment (Allen, 2012; de Roo, 2007). Understanding local government finance as a system implies that significant changes, such as new taxation powers or a new redistribution formula, would be implemented but also potentially restrained within a given system, and should not be considered in isolation. That insight also implies that the impacts of any given change are not likely to be linear or straightforward—and thus inflated claims will often be proved wrong.[2] The local government finance system includes the hard technical methods of accounting and budgets and meeting legal and bureaucratic requirements: but it also includes embedded practices and cultural assumptions that influence how any substantial change is absorbed and managed. Therefore, the contention in this research is that the local government finance discussion, and indeed all the agents involved in this complex arrangement – all of whom have a stake in resilient local government finance – would benefit from a whole system perspective.

Pike (2023), building on Copus et al. (2017), Newton and Karen (1985), Wilson and Game (2011), and Unlock Democracy (2021), outlines a broader typology of local government perspectives and paradigms that have emerged over the last century. He divides these into three typologies:

---

[2] This can be seen with the 2013 Business Rate Retention Scheme where incentives for growth did not materialise as planned.

1. The idea of the Sovereign Council—where local authorities generally have a degree of autonomy within a centrally defined system of governance.
2. New Public Management—where the state is rolled back (Peck & Tickell, 2002) and ideas of the market and managerialism are introduced to local government alongside performance indicators.
3. Network Governance—where local authorities work in partnership with wider networks in the private and civic sectors, where the relationship within central local relations is negotiated in self-organised systems.

There is considerable overlap in this typology. However, we believe the complex system perspective in this book sits best with the network conceptualisation, recognising that local government finance is a complex inter-territorial system of governance and practice involving networks of agents and stakeholders in a variety of sectors that emerge and evolve over time.

Complementing the system-based approach, we also mobilise recent engagement with conjunctural analysis, particularly ideas around critical junctures (Sorensen, 2023) where we argue that England is in the midst of an opportune moment to consider, influence, and deliver reform in the local government finance system following the election of a Labour government in 2024 with a 'mission driven' focus (Labour manifesto 2024). Conjunctural analysis is an emerging analysis framework that can trace its lineage back to the work of Gramsci and latterly Stuart Hall in the discipline of urban planning. More recently it has been deployed by Peck (2017a, 2017b) and Sorensen (2023) to analyse urban phenomena ranging from urban decline to the adoption of methods of land value capture. At its heart is the idea that system changes happen, and can be understood, "when a number of forces and contradictions, which are at work in different key practices and sites in a social formation, come together or 'con-join' in the same moment and political space" (Hall, 2011, p. 705).

Peck (2017a, p. 10) argued that to understand change, "it is important to consider issues of contextual, positional and situational specificity". It is for this reason that we have adopted the complex adaptive system conceptual framework, in attempting to understand local government finances across the intergovernmental system of working and stakeholder interaction. It enables understanding of the "reflexive interpretations and interplay between grounded circumstances, mediating conditions and contingent effects on the one hand, and their enabling conditions of existence, operational parameters and connective circuits on the other" (Peck, 2017a, p. 9).

Sorensen (2023) argues that critical junctures are closely related to, and can be seen in tandem with, theories of path dependence—because major institutions, in this case processes of local government finance, are typically long-held, sticky, and difficult to change. The critical juncture is the choice point (or the tipping point) when a new option is selected over an older way of working and, once deployed, is difficult to reverse. Sorensen (2023) and Hall (2016, p. 41) suggest that conjunctures of significant institutional change are relatively rare because "major institutional changes are likely to require exceptional circumstances, because change of this magnitude depends on coalitions that are especially difficult to build".

While the conjunctural method is typically used in retrospect to understand what has happened in a given situation, we deploy it in a slightly different manner, arguing that in the instance of local government finance in England, we are potentially in a 'conjunctural moment' where there is potential to bring about meaningful change in the operation of public finances. We therefore mobilise critical conjunctural theory to highlight the potential conditions for reform. An intersection of multiple processes and a coalition of political pressures for local government finance reform has coalesced around:

- An empty public purse.
- Local government in severe financial trouble.
- A new Labour Government emphasis on missions.
- Government imperative to rebuild public services.
- An audit/assurance system struggling to fulfil its duties.
- Continued pressure for devolution and place-based working.

All of these create combined momentum for pushing back against a path-dependent local government finance system that is often fearful of unintended consequences of reform. Capoccia and Kelemen (2007, p. 348) argue that critical junctures are "relatively short periods of time during which there is a substantially heightened probability that agents' choices will affect the outcome of interest". By mobilising the idea of critical junctures, it is possible to consider whereabouts England is within this process of change and direct resources towards positive change. A given critical juncture is typically conceived as a sequence of events (Sorensen, 2023; Soifer, 2012; Berins Collier & Collier, 1991) and is visualised in Fig. 2.1.

This sequence can be considered across five stages, read left to right. First, the antecedent conditions that shape current conditions and the available options in the critical juncture. Second, the permissive conditions that prepare the ground for major change. Third, the critical juncture itself, where choices are made around new ways of working. Fourth, the reactive sequence where the new way of working is resisted, refined, and adopted; and, fifth, outcomes where the new way of working is itself institutionalised.

This process can be applied to local government in England, as represented in Fig. 2.2.

In this case, the antecedent conditions are long held within the institutions of local government finance, in some respects dating back to the Poor Law in the 1600s and the more recent centralising tendency of government since the end of the Second World War, the more immediate

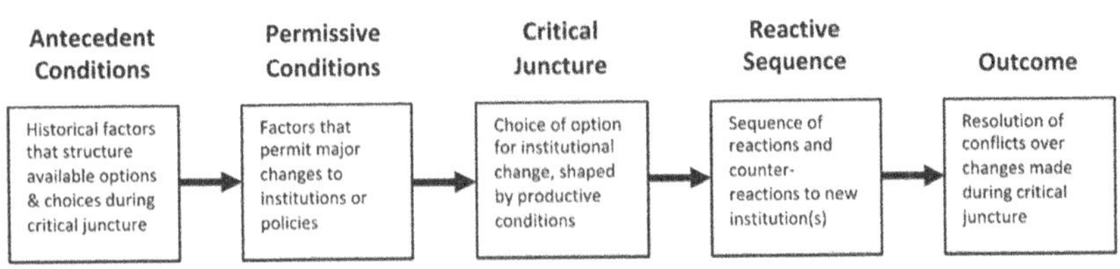

Fig. 2.1 The critical juncture sequence. (Source: Adapted from Mahoney, 2000 and Sorensen, 2023

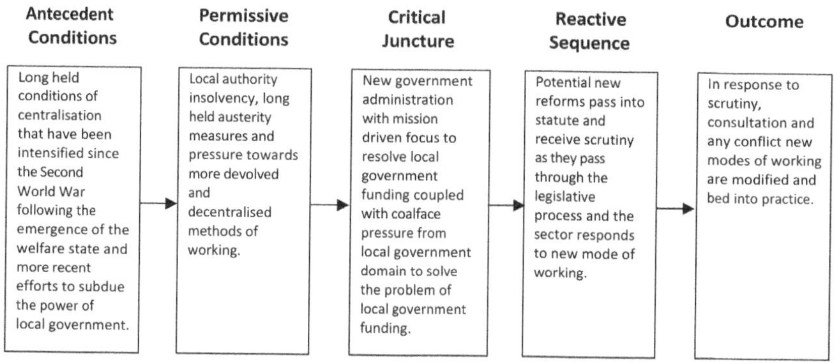

Fig. 2.2 Current local government finance critical juncture

conditions of austerity, and the parallel struggle to fund public services amid myriad pressures and conditions of uncertainty. The permissive conditions are the already highlighted public finance turmoil, individual local authority insolvency, the call for devolution and place-based budgeting, and the call for mission-based change in the perspective of government working. The critical juncture itself is perhaps yet to happen but England is well placed with the advantage of a new government with a commanding political majority. The new government's manifesto stressed partnership with local government at several points in the service of rebuilding public services, but in the knowledge that public funding is likely to remain tight in the 2020s. Equally, the government is faced with a sector in severe financial difficulty, with an eye to the political consequences of further service reductions, and authorities often lacking the financial and personnel capacity to act as effective partners. At the time of writing, England likely currently falls somewhere between permissive conditions and the potential for a critical juncture. This implies that debates in the next two years may decisively shape such a critical juncture and shape the proceeding reactive sequence and final output.

We return in Chap. 9 to further analyse the potential critical juncture in England in 2024–2025. The following chapter explores in more detail a range of system-wide influences that could be expected to frame decision-making by local government finance practitioners. These are a range, not necessarily comprehensive, of the types of structural features within political systems that determine how a state's local government finance system operates. The key insight is that these (and other) features of political systems differ between states—and thus the influences acting upon local government finance systems, and practitioners' responses to them, also differ between states.

Adopting a systems perspective implies a view of local government finance—and indeed local government—that is at odds with key aspects of the British political tradition (see Richards et al., 2024 for a discussion of this point). This tradition promotes the 'Westminster model' of strong majoritarian, power-hoarding governance, seeing this as the cornerstone of political stability (Vines, 2014; Marsh & Hall, 2007; Marsh et al., 2003). It is both "a political culture or body of beliefs widely held in British society" and "inscribed in the institutions and processes of British government" (Marsh & Hall, 2007, p. 221). The British Political Tradition prizes Parliamentary sovereignty, Ministerial accountability, and central discretionary powers, and is averse to rule-based practices and accepting multiple locations of legitimacy and political power.

In relation to the local government system, the BPT manifests in the form of what Bulpitt (1983) termed the 'dual polity'. This phrase denoted a system of territorial management operating through much of the twentieth century. Local government was permitted considerable discretion to act in its sphere of influence, allowing central government to take little notice of it. Bulpitt argued that the animating objective of this arrangement was 'central autonomy' (Bradbury, 2006). That is, the UK government's aim was to avoid ongoing relationships with local authorities, to concentrate on 'high politics'.

This divide began to break down through the 1980s, as economic and political pressures mounted on the centre to intervene in local government. But the key assumptions of the dual polity endured (Carmichael, 1996) and remain to this day. Ongoing central-local relations are limited. The UK government retains vast reserve powers to intervene in local authority operations, to fund or not to fund them, and to add and remove legal duties. Ironically, this perspective is also visible in many recent demands from the sector, and supportive commentators, for fiscal autonomy and additional powers. Few such contributions address in any detail central–local relationships, accountability mechanisms, or systems to manage failure—even though these would be unavoidable, and significant, features of any 'reform'. The upshot can be that centre and localities talk past each other to demand powers and money irrespective of any wider system effects.

A key theme of this book is to highlight that the terms of this type of debate are very different in other countries. Our three non-Anglo-Saxon case studies facilitate practices that align better with complex systems: multiple poles of justiciable power and rights, and thus parity of esteem; transparent statutory systems; limited discretion, often exercised by agreement; balancing local revenue choices with sufficiency of funding; audit and propriety check by independent institutions; and a formal/statutory forum for dispute resolution. Local authorities in these locations do indeed have greater fiscal powers than their English counterparts—but they exercise their powers within a nation-wide system of governance exhibiting a rule-based approach to relationships, independent regulatory institutions, and legal backing. Understanding the interlocking effects of these features of the systems can also answer the charge that any change to the English system that simply 'imported' a single feature of another country's practices would fail.

We describe the approach of these case studies to central-local relations, in the form of their financial arrangements, as 'embedded autonomy'. Because this approach is distinct from most previous debate in England, understanding it more fully allows us to move beyond some of the fixed dualities that dominate debate over local government finance (and indeed devolution of power) in England. For instance, local authorities' discretion and ability to act are not necessarily a function of whether they are financially self-sufficient. Local autonomy need not be measured by the extent, or absence, of audit, reporting, and transparency requirements. Local government discretion and capacity, and central government's ability to deliver on its electoral mandate, are not necessarily a zero-sum game. And the flexibility of a system, and its capacity to respond to crises, is not necessarily reliant on limitless central reserve powers. We return to the concept of embedded autonomy in Chap. 9.

References

Allen, P. M. (2012). Cities: The visible expression of co evolving complexity. In J. Portugali, H. Meyer, E. Stolk, & T. Ekim (Eds.), *Complexity theories of cities have come of age* (pp. 67–89). Springer.

Arnold, C. A. (2010). Adaptive watershed planning and climate change. *Environmental and Energy Law and Policy Journal, 5*(2), 417–487.

Berins Collier, R., & Collier, D. (1991). *Shaping the political arena*. Princeton University Press.

Bovaird, T. (2008). Emergent strategic management and planning mechanisms in complex adaptive systems: The case of the UK best value initiative. *Public Management Review, 10*(3), 319–340. https://doi.org/10.1080/14719030802002741

Bradbury, J. (2006). *Territory and power* revisited: Theorising territorial politics in the United Kingdom after devolution. *Political Studies, 54*(3), 559–582. https://doi.org/10.1111/j.1467-9248.2006.00615

Bulpitt, J. (1983). *Territory and power in the United Kingdom*. Manchester University Press.

Capoccia, G., & Kelemen, R. D. (2007). The study of critical junctures: Theory, narrative, and counterfactuals in historical institutionalism. *World Politics, 59*(3), 341–369. https://doi.org/10.1017/S0043887100020852

Carmichael, P. (1996). The changing territorial operating code of the United Kingdom: Evidence from Northern Ireland. *Public Administration, 74*(3), 413–433. https://doi.org/10.1111/j.1467-9299.1996.tb00878.x

Copus, C., Roberts, M., & Wall, R. (2017). *Local government in England: Centralisation, autonomy and control*. Palgrave Macmillan.

de Roo, G. (2007). Shifts in planning practice and theory: From a functional towards a communicative rationale. In G. de Roo & G. Porter (Eds.), *Fuzzy planning: The role of actors in a fuzzy governance environment* (pp. 103–114). Ashgate.

Demos. (2024). *Liberated public services: A new vision for citizens, professionals and policy makers*. Demos.

Dietz, T., Ostrom, E., & Stern, P. C. (2003). The struggle to govern the commons. *Science, 302*(5652), 1907–1912. https://doi.org/10.1126/science.1091015

Foster, C. D., Jackman, R., & Perlman, M. (1980). *Local government finance in a unitary state*. George Allen and Unwin.

French, M., Hesselgreaves, H., Wilson, R., Hawkins, M., & Lowe, T. (2023). *Harnessing complexity for better outcomes in public and not-for-profit services.* Bristol University Press.

Geyer, R., & Cairney, P. (2015). *Handbook on complexity and public policy.* Edward Elgar.

Geyer, R., & Rihani, S. (2010). *Complexity and public policy: A new approach to 21st Century politics, policy and society.* Routledge.

Haasnoot, M., Kwakkel, J. H., Walker, W. E., & ter Maat, J. (2013). Dynamic adaptive policy pathways: A method for crafting robust decisions for a deeply uncertain world. *Global Environmental Change, 23*(2), 485–498. https://doi.org/10.1016/j.gloenvcha.2012.12.006

Hall, P. A. (2016). Politics as a process structured in space and time. In K. O. Fioretos, T. G. Falleti, & A. D. Sheingate (Eds.), *The Oxford handbook of historical institutionalism* (pp. 31–50). Oxford University Press.

Hall, S. (2011). The neo-liberal revolution. *Cultural Studies, 25*(6), 705–728. https://doi.org/10.1080/09502386.2011.619886

Institute for Fiscal Studies. (2024). *How have English councils' funding and spending changed? 2010 to 2024.* IFS.

Kato, S., & Ahern, J. (2008). Learning by doing: Adaptive planning as a strategy to address uncertainty in planning. *Journal of Environmental Planning and Management, 51*(4), 543–559. https://doi.org/10.1080/09640560802117028

Keith-Lucas, B., & Richards, P. G. (1978). *A history of local government in the twentieth century.* Routledge.

Klijn, E. H. (2008). Complexity theory and public administration: What's new? Key concepts in complexity theory compared to their counterparts in public administration research. *Public Management Review, 10*(3), 299–317. https://doi.org/10.1080/14719030802002675

Lowe, T., French, M., Hawkins, M., Hesselgreaves, H., & Wilson, R. (2021). New development: Responding to complexity in public services—the human learning systems approach. *Public Money & Management, 41*(7), 573–576. https://doi.org/10.1080/09540962.2020.1832738

Mahoney, J. (2000) Path dependence in historical sociology. *Theory and Society, 29*(4), 507–548. https://www.jstor.org/stable/3108585

Marsh, D., & Hall, M. (2007). The British political tradition: Explaining the fate of new Labour's constitutional reform agenda. *British Politics, 2*, 215–238. https://doi.org/10.1057/palgrave.bp.4200055

Marsh, D., Richards, D., & Smith, M. (2003). Unequal plurality: Towards an asymmetric power model of British politics. *Government and Opposition, 38*(3), 306–322. https://doi.org/10.1111/1477-7053.t01-1-00017

Newton, K., & Karen, T. J. (1985). *The politics of local expenditure*. Macmillan.

Patterson, T. M., Niccolucci, V., & Marchettini, N. (2008). Adaptive environmental management of tourism in the province of Siena, Italy using the ecological footprint. *Journal of Environmental Management, 86*(2), 407–418. https://doi.org/10.1016/j.jenvman.2006.04.017

Peck, J. (2017a). Transatlantic city, part 1: Conjunctural urbanism. *Urban Studies, 54*(1), 4–30. https://doi.org/10.1177/0042098016679355

Peck, J. (2017b). Transatlantic city, part 2: Late entrepreneurialism. *Urban Studies, 54*(2), 327–363. https://doi.org/10.1177/0042098016683859

Peck, J., & Tickell, A. (2002). A neoliberalizing space. *Antipode, 34*(3), 380–404. https://doi.org/10.1111/1467-8330.00247

Pike, A. (2023). *Financialization and local statecraft*. Oxford University Press—United Kingdom.

Preiser, R. (2018). *Key features of complex adaptive systems: And practical implications for guiding action*. CST Policy Brief 2018.

Richards, D., Smith, M. J., Warner, S., & Marsh, D. (2024). 'Crisis what crisis?' Understanding the recurring problems of the British state. *British Journal of Politics and International Relations, 0*(0)—on-line first. https://doi.org/10.1177/13691481241269329.

Rhodes, M. L., & MacKechnie, G. (2003). Understanding public service systems: Is there a role for complex adaptive systems theory? *Emergence, 5*(4), 57–85. https://doi.org/10.1207/s15327000em0504_6

Sengupta, U., Rauws, S. W., & de Roo, G. (2016). Planning and complexity: Engaging with temporal dynamics, uncertainty and complex adaptive systems. *Environment and Planning B: Planning and Design, 43*(6), 970–974. https://doi.org/10.1177/0265813516675872

Skrimizea, E., Haniotou, H., & Parra, C. (2018). On the "complexity turn" in planning: An adaptive rationale to navigate spaces and times of uncertainty. *Planning Theory, 18*(1), 122–142. https://doi.org/10.1177/1473095218780515

Soifer, H. D. (2012). The causal logic of critical junctures. *Comparative Political Studies, 45*(12), 1572–1597. https://doi.org/10.1177/0010414012463902

Sorensen, A. (2023). Urban intensification and land value capture in Toronto: Conjunctural analysis, critical junctures, and developmental pathways in urban planning. *Environment and Planning A: Economy and Space, 0*(0)—Online First. https://doi.org/10.1177/0308518X231216535.

Unlock Democracy. (2021). *Local government in England: Forty years of decline*. Unlock Democracy.

van Buuren, A., Driessen, P. P. J., Rijswick, M. V., Rietveld, P., Salet, W., Spit, T., & Teisman, G. (2013). Towards adaptive spatial planning for climate change: Balancing between robustness and flexibility. *Journal for European Environmental & Planning Law, 10*(1), 29–53. https://doi.org/10.1163/18760104-01001003.

Vines, E. (2014). Reframing *English nationalism and Euroscepticism*: From populism to the British political tradition. *British Politics, 9*(3), 255–274. https://doi.org/10.1057/bp.2014.3

Westley, F. (2002). The devil in the dynamics: Adaptive management on the front lines. In L. Gunderson & C. S. Holling (Eds.), *Panarchy: Understanding transformations in human and natural systems* (pp. 333–360). Island Press.

Wilson, D., & Game, C. (2011). *Local government in the United Kingdom* (5th ed.). Palgrave Macmillan.

Zellner, M., & Campbell, S. D. (2015). Planning for deep-rooted problems: What can we learn from aligning complex systems and wicked problems? *Planning Theory & Practice, 16*(4), 457–478. https://doi.org/10.1080/14649357.2015.1084360

3

Applying a Systems Perspective to Local Government Finance

In this chapter, we consider the system-wide influences that frame and help shape local government finance practice. We set out influences that emerge from constitutional imperatives: the different forms that central–local relationships can take. We then explore the impact of politics: key changes to local government finance policy in England since 2010, summarising the discernible effects of these changes. Next, we reference scholarly literature on financialisation—the reworking of policy decision-making in the interests of mobile capital. This chapter then outlines the research project from which this book emerged. The following chapters then describe the local government finance system of England, followed by Germany, Italy, and Japan.

Central–Local Relations

Local authorities face restrictions on their financial freedom that do not apply to nation-states. They cover comparatively small populations and geographical areas; they exercise specified legal duties; and they face legal controls over revenue raising and management. The influence of those

K. Muldoon-Smith et al., *Embedded Autonomy*,
https://doi.org/10.1007/978-981-97-9030-2_3

contexts has been investigated by multiple academic literatures. The literature on fiscal federalism and multilevel governance has explored how local authority finance systems can derive from national equity and citizenship concerns, ranging from public choice perspectives (Tiebout, 1956) to perspectives focusing on offsetting citizens' ability to pay with a redistribution system (Musgrave, 1959).

A state's position on these matters can significantly influence how exposed local authority finance is to variations in economic performance between areas (and at different time periods). Central governments may also seek to intervene in, influence, and induce local authority behaviour in line with equity and citizenship imperatives; or to attempt to ensure that national political goals are realised. Central–local relationships can, therefore, take the form of contractual relationships between governments within a state, either transactional (with defined outcomes) or relational (committing to cooperation) (Charbit, 2020). Alternatively, a central government may provide financial or legal inducements to outsource functions to private providers (Ferry & Eckersley, 2020; Lowndes & Gardner, 2016), with the aim of saving money. Central governments may also use earmarked grants in order to compel or induce local authorities to spend fixed or minimum amounts of funding on specific duties (Smith, 2007).

In some states, local authorities have taken a path of 'urban entrepreneurialism'—emphasising economic policy as an equal concern to public service delivery. This can lead to the privileging of market values, promoting "collaborative efforts with market actors and engaging global markets and agendas, and the use of state powers to promote and protect municipal investments" (Deas et al., 2020; Fuller, 2018). Central–local relations also embody differing interpretations of public accountability. Some states may require formal reporting from local authorities against spending programmes, on the grounds that the central government is acting for the 'principal' (the national electorate) in holding the local authority (the 'agent') to account for its actions. In other states, accountability may be primarily political, with an independent organisation, such as a national audit body, responsible for ensuring financial probity and imposing penalties or controls where it has been absent. This requirement can be implemented through a variety of mechanisms: transparency, external audit, and regulation of financial management (Ferry et al., 2015; Hood, 2010; Murphy et al., 2019).

The influence of legal and institutional frameworks has heightened significance during periods of 'austerity', as experienced by English local authorities since 2010. Innovative institutional responses to challenging situations (Kim & Warner, 2020; Lowndes & McCaughie, 2013) cannot avoid being shaped by the quantity—and as importantly, the source—of funding available to the local state. Local authorities unable to influence legal frameworks would naturally turn their attention to mechanisms of available local government funding (non-statutory in England). This ostensibly technical matter 'plays an outsized, but often overlooked, role in the urban process' (Tapp & Kay, 2019).

The influence of national political and administrative frameworks upon public services and local authority roles has often been neglected by recent political debate in England. Within this, the shape of the local government finance system comprises a pattern of incentives that shape authorities' behaviour. Local government finance systems are historically contingent, normally overlaid on former systems, and thus are rarely coherently designed. They can therefore embody incentive patterns derived from a mish-mash of decades of alterations, driven by ephemeral imperatives. Thus, while a central government may declare that it seeks a fundamental reset (for instance) in central–local relations, it can be undermined by a finance system that points local authorities in multiple directions that conflict with the stated intention.

For instance, an authority receiving much of its income from tied grants will tend to (or be required to) prioritise the policy areas associated with those grants. One receiving much of its income from volatile local taxes may be conservative in its service provision. Another may have much freer access to capital than to revenue funding and may prioritise infrastructure-based policies and recycle revenue (e.g., transport fares, property rents) to service provision. Another might derive substantial revenue from income or corporation taxes, and thus pursue a policy aim of increasing its tax base by making the locality attractive for companies and individuals seeking to relocate.

All real-world funding systems carry within them a perspective on the balance between equity and fiscal autonomy; the nature of accountability;

and the balance between the importance of service delivery and economic management. This suggests that complex interactions between methods of funding and structures of governance over time inform the development of territory and space—they are co-evolutionary and path dependent. All countries that fund public services through grant and tax exhibit this complex interaction. Just as infrastructure underpins the spaces and places of public life, the system of local government funding helps define how these locations are (un)developed and supported.

For example, in England, every school built, space maintained, or public health emergency mitigated emerges via a public funding mechanism, a source of income, and a decision to spend (or not). This fiscal 'decision space' delivers an alternative way of understanding how territories develop and how societies have access to and utilise spaces within these locations. Central–local relations, financial management, and sources of revenue—bounded within central–local tensions and the relative performance of funding mechanisms—play a central, but often occluded, role in regulating territorial investment and structuring urban change. Territories are therefore, in part, defined by the imprint of the path-dependent funding institutions that produce them.

Moreover, studying local government finance also provides a lens to consider and examine wider questions of what local government is for and how it is currently constituted. In England, the traditional method of central government redistribution and equalisation between locations has been replaced with a greater emphasis on self-sufficiency and entrepreneurism—continuing a theme emerging in the 1980s and 1990s of local government managerialism and efficiency. Under these conditions, it is unsurprising that practitioner and policy attention has clustered around ideas for new sources of finance, in order to obtain more money.

Recent Government Reform: A Critical Perspective

The UK government established a number of reforms to English local government funding during the 2010s. The underlying policy objective was to increase local authorities' control over their own financial health, but their effect has been constrained. The 2010s has seen some reduction in ring-fencing of transfer grants, and a tacit encouragement of commercial property development. But the substantial reduction in transfer grants outlined in the introduction has reduced local authorities' control over their financial health. A policy that nominally increases local accountability has, in practice, been accompanied by severe service reductions (Kim & Warner, 2020; Lowndes & Gardner, 2016).

In principle, local revenue-raising could compensate for some of these reductions. However, English local authorities have also seen restrictions on raising domestic property tax—the government traditionally sets a limit in the region of 2–4% each year. Consequently, their total revenues have been unable to keep pace with costs and identified need (Institute for Fiscal Studies, 2024) even where maximal tax increases are the norm—for instance, virtually all local authorities made the decision during 2023–2024 to increase council tax by the maximum 4% (Holland, 2024). In parallel, business rate payments have been sought far more assiduously from properties previously rarely held to be liable: for instance, agricultural land with occasional use (such as festivals for a few weeks per year) and automatic teller machines (before a Supreme Court decision banned this in 2018). The headline rates of both taxes rise year on year, increasing taxpayer disquiet and potentially eroding the legitimacy of both taxes in the long term.

The UK government has also attempted to draw closer links between local authorities' policy decisions and their revenue levels. It reformed the non-domestic rating system in England in 2013, permitting local authorities to retain up to 50% of the increase in rate revenue against a 2013 baseline (Mor & Sandford, 2017; Muldoon-Smith & Greenhalgh, 2015). The purpose was to incentivise local authorities to grow their local economy and benefit financially from a resulting increase in business rate revenues. However, the system features several shortcomings. It assumes a link—between local gross value added (GVA)[1] and property rateable value—which research demonstrates to be low to non-existent (Mor & Sandford, 2017; Muldoon-Smith & Greenhalgh, 2015). The

[1] Gross value added (GVA) is the measurement of the value of goods and services produced in an area, industry, or sector of an economy.

implementation of the policy provides limited incentives for local authorities: as the UK government retains control over the valuation of property and the tax rate, the only source of growth is building additional commercial property rather than to attract or grow high-value firms. This incentive is available only to a minority of premium authorities, contingent on the sectoral structure of their economies and the availability of land. Even those authorities that can grow revenue in this way see it mitigated by a redistribution mechanism (the tariff and top-up system) designed to ensure that less wealthy authorities can meet their statutory duties (Mor & Sandford, 2017) and the liability associated with unresolved rateable value appeals (Greenhalgh et al., 2016).

The web of incentives plays well to lower tier authorities in the South-East of England outside main urban areas with robust economies and space to build (Bates, 2018), and to some extent buoyant Northern cities. Other locations, such as buoyant city economies lacking space to build, benefit far less if at all from their economic success (Muldoon-Smith & Greenhalgh, 2015). Thus, the centrally designed local government finance system has created inconsistent incentives to pursue growth in productivity and innovation across different locations.

This is a manifestation of a more pervasive conundrum within local authority finance: how to balance imperatives toward territorial equity and redistribution, local accountability for local public spending and the wider concern for certainty in the overall local government finance system, and at the scale of each local authority. These principles often end up working against each other: for example, when a local authority receives substantial transfer grants to compensate for a shortfall in local revenue, local financial accountability is reduced. This conundrum is inherent in the fiscal federalism literature (Musgrave, 1959; Oates, 1972; Tiebout, 1956), but it rarely features in public accountancy research or in political debate. The balance between these principles governs the sources of any individual local authority's funding and thus strongly influences its policy choices.

In addition, the distinction between capital and revenue accounting has generated specific pressures in England during the 2010s. Faced with multiple constraints on their use of revenue spending, many English authorities have pursued an area in which they are relatively unconstrained by law: investment of capital funds, often in commercial property, to raise revenue (Christophers, 2018; Pike et al., 2019). The logic is simple: UK authorities have been able to borrow at near-sovereign rates, purchase commercial property, and rent it out for a net profit; the profit constitutes revenue funding and can be reinvested in services. This activity overlaps with the conventional purchase of buildings in order to de-risk development opportunities, which subsequently incentivises new development and wider urban regeneration. The government has welcomed the inherent entrepreneurialism around property investment while tightening up statutory codes of practice and scrutiny to discourage borrowing for investment alone (National Audit Office, 2020; Sandford, 2020).

Financialisation: A Red Herring?

In a context of fiscal tightening and local authority solvency, narratives of devolution and decentralisation have prefigured notions of local responsibility for service provision. There has been far less consideration of how funding frameworks underpin this situation—instruments and revenue sources frame the local responsibility for service provision and decisions around placed-based objectives. Studies of this question focus most frequently on the conceptual framework of 'financialisation': the increasing dominance of financial actors, markets, practices, measurements, and narratives at various scales, resulting in a structural transformation of economies, firms, states, and households (Aalbers, 2015). Fields (2018, p. 119) defined financialisation as "an idea that has taken hold as a means of understanding the distinctive role of finance in contemporary capitalism, and its influence on space, the economy, governance and everyday life".

This framework suggests that local governments' policy priorities, individual investment or asset-related decisions, and thus the delivery of public service commitments are increasingly determined by the financial priorities of private sector funding sources and intermediaries. Alternatively, local authorities may seek to use financial vehicles—joint ventures, special purpose vehicles—to seek additional revenue themselves. Inspired by the work of Weber (2010) and Peck and Whiteside (2016), Lin et al. (2019, p. 436) indicate that some "American and European local governments have become reliant upon financial instruments to repackage and reschedule current fiscal problems temporarily by selling off city futures". Novel financial incentives can also influence approaches to service provision: several authors have highlighted the influence of funders in the delivery of Social Impact Bonds (SIBs) during the 2010s (Fraser et al., 2018; Edmiston & Nichols, 2018; Kim & Warner, 2020). However, Lin et al. (2019) concede that it remains "controversial and vague how the transformative process of financialisation has played out in different geopolitical and economic contexts" (p. 347). This is echoed by Peck and Whiteside (2016, p. 238) who caution that financialisation is "pervasive in reach yet uneven in effect" and Pike (2023) who demonstrated that financialisation has had only minimal impact on local government practice in England.

The concept of financialisation has connected into debates of decentralised government provision (Rodríguez-Pose & Gill, 2003) and 'roll back' and 'roll out' neo-liberalism (Peck, 2010; Peck & Tickell, 2002). Moreover, in England, it has provided new insight into how local places and government adapt to measures of austerity introduced since 2010 (Christophers, 2018; Gray & Barford, 2018; MacKinnon, 2015) and some of the controversies associated with these efforts, such as the use of Lender Option Borrower Option (LOBO) loans (Mertens et al., 2019). However, we suggest that financialisation has had a peripheral influence on English local authorities' decision-making. The optimal market conditions for substantial investor returns rarely exist: they are typically found only in major premium locations that are bounded within and undergirded by assistive rental conditions such as Central London, New York, or Frankfurt and secondary cities such as Chicago and Manchester. Such locations are bountiful but form a narrow striation in the overall territorial expanse (see Muldoon-Smith and Sandford (2021) for a more detailed account of this situation).

Bound up within this simplification is the often-uncritical contention that territories are establishing and exploiting regulations and policy instruments to smooth the flow of investment into the built environments of cities, and that financial and policy decisions are reshaped to take advantage of this phenomenon. The more common reality is locations with inferior income conditions are simply bypassed by financial flows (Muldoon-Smith & Greenhalgh, 2015). Such locations are left reliant on more local methods and conventional sources of income. It is therefore important to have a critical perspective of the situation in the 'everywhere else' that forms the vast majority of England's territorial development, to understand how economically uneven territories have developed through the structuring influence of local government finance.

In summary, the windows of opportunity for financialisation in English local government are few and far between. This is due to central–local relations, public service equity considerations, and the regulatory framework. Instead, we argue that tensions within central–local relationships (between autonomy and control), and the operation of the overall local government finance system, is more pertinent to the funding behaviour of local authorities. The perspective adopted in this book attempts to provide a first staging post for a more longstanding engagement with local government finance—one that pushes back against the tendency for matters of local authority finance to only gain public exposure when there are questions of solvency and the potential for bankruptcy in any state.

The Project

Local government finance is therefore subject to multiple influences—from administrative interactions and legal requirements set by more powerful political actors at state (or regional) level, from market forces, and from national political imperatives. The influence from this multiplicity of factors plays out across a state's system of local government. Local authorities do not simply obtain money, seek more, and then deliver services: they operate in a complex web of relationships. This insight is natural to practitioners, but it is belied by the simplicity of some recent calls for reform in England.

To reflect upon the root situation in England, the following four chapters provide a more in-depth understanding of the systems of local government finance, firstly in England, followed by Germany, Italy, and

Japan. These latter three countries were selected for two reasons. First, all feature local authorities with broad responsibilities, a wide range of revenue-raising powers, and an established role within the territorial governance of the state. Elements of practice within those countries—for instance, specific taxation powers—are frequently presented as options for change in the English context. Second, these countries are all non-Anglophone. Local government and local government finance systems in Anglophone countries have a common ancestor in English practice and share many historical similarities. These include local revenue consisting primarily of property taxes; a lack of constitutional protection; limited functions; and more restrained legal or financial supervision by central officials.

It is hoped that examining the operation of these alternative systems will provide new contextual information for future proposals to reform the local government finance system in England. The selection of these countries grew out of a recognition that there are enough similarities to group them together (each have a decentralised system of local government finance, fixed reference points for local government working, and a national oversight regime) and acknowledgement that there are enough differences (Germany has a long history of decentralisation and federalism while Japan and Italy have more recently transitioned from centralised systems) to warrant comparative analysis in order to provoke debate around potential change in England. Examples of isolated practices that can be seen in each of the case studies have been featured at points in the English debate; for instance, tax powers and shared revenues in Japan (Kimura, 2015; Bessho, 2016; Centre for Cities, 2019), and redistribution in Germany (Werner, 2018; Bullerjahn & Thöne, 2020). However, we are not aware of any analysis (in English) of these systems as systems. Without such understanding, it is not easy to comprehend the role and significance of individual elements of these systems, how they interact, and, in turn, how they could inform new practices in England.

Previous examinations of international local government finance have typically drawnout features that are exotic by Anglophone standards. That approach provides little sense of how those features operate in the originating national context and financial system, nor how they can be compared to the local government finance system in England. This project is the first known recursive application of such research to the system in England, to inform potential reform. The system focus will provide new understanding for practitioners, policy makers, and academics engaged with the financing of local services and those seeking a broader understanding of sub-national governance systems and their relationship with the state and politics. The intention is that the insights in the research can be taken forward by local government practitioners and policy makers to help to articulate how new approaches to local government finances could be implemented effectively in England. In turn, the same insights have relevance for the international research locations, which may not have adopted a system-wide perspective before, and indeed any international location that is struggling to finance the increasing demand on local services.

This project examined the following features in each country:

- The structure of sub-national governance
- Local authority functions
- The regulatory regime
- Capital finance
- Sources of income
- Degree of own budgeting and accounting
- Method of territorial equalisation

While the book repeatedly emphasises several of these themes in Chaps. 4, 5, 6, and 7, particularly taking time to set out the roles and responsibilities of local authorities in detail in the different states, this is done to clarify the framework within which sources of finance operate. In each international location, a rule-based undergirding and associated clarity of vision for local government is seen as central to successful local government financing. This can be seen in stark contrast to the discretionary, ambiguous, and largely unwritten situation in England. While the rule-based accountancy system that governs local government finance is understandably prescriptive, there is far less detail and substantiation for what local government should do in the broadest sense, in respect to responsibilities held by other tiers of government, which roles are statutory and discretionary, and what the minimum provision and quality of service should be.

Methodology

A mixed research methodology has been developed and utilised within a cross-disciplinary perspective, blending insights from policy, territorial governance, finance, and real estate studies. Taken together, the empirical and secondary information products lay the foundation for creating a total system perspective of each location that is rarely seen in international literature.

The research has been foregrounded by a survey of a local government finance in England sent to senior officers in every local authority, receiving 160 responses and representing a variety of council types, every region in England, and councils with different political control. The foundation of the empirical research is a multi-phase interview process. During the course of the research, more than 80 respondents have been interviewed either individually or via panel discussion. Respondents were identified in each study location based on their expert knowledge (derived from experience in various tiers of government, oversight organisations, and academia) of the respective local government finance systems. Identifying respondents in each location was not straightforward due to the relative dearth of stakeholders with system-wide knowledge and the generally hidden nature of the sector. To overcome this issue, the research made use of knowledge brokers including the Local Government Information Unit, the Japan Local Government Centre in London, and the Chartered Institute of Public Finance and Accountancy.

The interview process included:

- Initial scoping interviews to provide context for the research and direction towards relevant resources and information on practice within the local government finance system in England.
- Subsequent scoping interviews with local government finance experts in the study locations to provide context and direction to relevant information sources.
- The research team then returned to the respondents in the respective study locations with findings, to cross-reference and sense-check the evidence leading to a valuable process of draft refinement and gap analysis.

- The research team then conducted a variety of panel[2] meetings with experts in England to highlight how the international findings could be applied in this context and to highlight opportunities for dissemination and policy impact.

Alongside interaction with the stakeholders in each location, the team examined information from secondary academic literature, government documentation and legislation regarding the legal structures and institutions underlying local government finance systems in Germany, Italy, and Japan. Concurrently, data was sourced from Government ministries and allied organisations to reflect the quantity and proportion of income sources in each location and to provide an opportunity for comparison. In England, obtaining detailed, accurate, and consistent information on the operation of local government finance systems was complicated, with sources sometimes providing contradictory information. In such cases, experts in each country were used as a validating mechanism for stress testing the information sources. In all cases the latest data was used alongside a criterion of consistency and detail. In the vast majority of cases this led the team to use the latest available data. In our analysis, we have tried to avoid selective reading of the case studies from afar, attempting to avoid only selecting instances that justify reform in England. To achieve this, we returned to respondents in each country and asked them to stress-test our arguments for sensitivity, accuracy, and bias.

References

Aalbers, M. B. (2015). The potential for financialization. *Dialogues in Human Geography*, *5*(2), 214–219. https://doi.org/10.1177/2043820615588158

Bates, D. (2018) *Business rate growth 2017–18*. https://www.linkedin.com/pulse/business-rates-growth-201718-dan-bates/?articleId=6472949282805673984.

[2] These panel meetings were both formal and informal, organised by the Local Government Information Unit or a by-product of training sessions organised by the same organisation.

Bessho, S.-I. (2016). *Case study of central and local government finance in Japan.* Asian Development Bank Institute.
Bullerjahn, M., & Thöne, J. (2020). *Municipal finance and municipal financial equalisation in Germany.* Deutsche Gesellscha für Internationale Zusammenarbeit (GIZ) GmbH.
Centre for Cities. (2019). *What does Japan tell us about the potential for fiscal devolution?* Centre for Cities.
Charbit, C. (2020). From "de jure" to "de facto" decentralised public policies: The multi-level governance approach. *The British Journal of Politics and International Relations, 22*(4), 809–819. https://doi.org/10.1177/1369148120937624
Christophers, B. (2018). *The new enclosure: The appropriation of public land in neoliberal Britain.* Verso.
Deas, I., Haughton, G., & Ward, K. (2020). Scalar postpolitics, inclusive growth and inclusive economies: Challenging the greater Manchester agglomeration model. *Cambridge Journal of Regions, Economy and Society.* https://doi.org/10.1093/cjres/rsaa022
Edmiston, D., & Nichols, A. (2018). Social impact bonds: The role of private capital in outcome-based commissioning. *Journal of Social Policy, 47*(1), 57–76. https://doi.org/10.1017/S0047279417000125
Ferry, L., & Eckersley, P. (2020). Hybridizing the institutional logics of performance improvement and budgetary stewardship in English and welsh local government. *Public Policy and Administration, 35*(1), 45–64. https://doi.org/10.1177/0952076718781433
Ferry, L., Eckersley, P., & Zakaria, Z. (2015). Accountability and transparency in English local government: Moving from matching parts to awkward couple? *Financial Accountability and Management, 31*(3), 345–361. https://doi.org/10.1111/faam.12060
Fields, D. (2018). Constructing a new asset class: Property-led financial accumulation after the crisis. *Economic Geography, 94*(2), 118–140. https://doi.org/10.1080/00130095.2017.1397492
Fraser, A., Tan, S., Lagarde, M., & Mays, N. (2018). Narratives of promise, narratives of caution: A review of the literature on social impact bonds. *Social Policy and Administration, 52*(1), 4–28. https://doi.org/10.1111/spol.12260
Fuller, C. (2018). Entrepreneurial urbanism, austerity and economic governance. *Cambridge Journal of Regions, Economy and Society, 11*(3), 565–585. https://doi.org/10.1093/cjres/rsy023

Gray, M., & Barford, A. (2018). The depths of the cuts: The uneven geography of local government austerity. *Cambridge Journal of Regions, Economy and Society, 11*(3), 541–563. https://doi.org/10.1093/cjres/rsy019

Greenhalgh, P., Muldoon-Smith, K., & Angus, S. (2016). Commercial property tax in the UK: Business rates and rating appeals. *Journal of Property Investment and Finance, 34*(6), 602–619. https://doi.org/10.1108/JPIF-03-2016-0014

Holland, J. (2024) *Governments use of exceptional financial support at best careless and maybe reckless*. Room151. Retrieved June 13, 2024, from https://www.room151.co.uk/funding/exceptional-financial-support-careless-reckless/

Hood, C. (2010). Accountability and transparency: Siamese twins, matching parts, awkward couple? *West European Politics, 33*(5), 989–1009. https://doi.org/10.1080/01402382.2010.486122

Institute for Fiscal Studies. (2024). *How have English councils' funding and spending changed? 2010 to 2024*. IFS.

Kim, Y., & Warner, M. (2020). Pragmatic municipalism or austerity urbanism? Understanding local government responses to fiscal stress. *Local Government Studies*. https://doi.org/10.1080/03003930.2020.1729751

Kimura, S. (2015). Goals and reforms of the current Japanese local tax system. *Hitotsubashi Journal of Law and Politics, 43*, 17–48.

Lin, G. C. S., Smart, A., Li, X., & Hu, F. Z. Y. (2019). Financializing Chinese cities: State–capital nexus and the uneven geography of housing speculation. *Area Development and Policy, 4*(4), 435–453. https://doi.org/10.1080/23792949.2019.1625277

Lowndes, V., & Gardner, A. (2016). Local governance under the conservatives: Super-austerity, devolution and the 'smarter state'. *Local Government Studies, 42*(3), 357–375. https://doi.org/10.1080/03003930.2016.1150837

Lowndes, V., & McCaughie, K. (2013). Weathering the perfect storm? Austerity and institutional resilience in local government. *Politics & Policy, 41*(4), 533–549. https://doi.org/10.1332/030557312X655747

MacKinnon, D. (2015). Devolution, state restructuring and policy divergence in the UK. *The Geographical Journal, 181*(1), 47–56. https://doi.org/10.1111/geoj.12057

Mertens, A., Trampusch, C., Fastenrath, F., & Wangemann, R. (2019). The political economy of local government financialization and the role of policy diffusion. *Regulation and Governance*. https://doi.org/10.1111/rego.12285

Mor, F., & Sandford, M. (2017). Growing pains: Property taxation and revenue incentives in English local government. *Local Economy, 32*(5), 399–419. https://doi.org/10.1177/0269094217720738

Muldoon-Smith, K., & Greenhalgh, P. (2015). Passing the buck without the bucks: Some reflections on fiscal decentralisation and the business rate retention scheme in England. *Local Economy, 30*(6), 609–626. https://doi.org/10.1177/0269094215599724

Muldoon-Smith, K., & Sandford, M. (2021). Grasping the nettle: The central–local constraints on local government funding in England. *Territory, Politics, Governance, 1-18*. https://doi.org/10.1080/21622671.2021.1924249

Murphy, P., Ferry, L., Glennon, R., & Greenhalgh, K. (2019). *Public service accountability: Rekindling a debate*. United Kingdom.

Musgrave, R. (1959). *The theory of public finance*. McGraw-Hill.

National Audit Office. (2020). *Local authority investment in commercial property*. National Audit Office.

Oates, W. (1972). *Fiscal federalism*. Edward Elgar.

Peck, J. (2010). *Constructions of neoliberal reason*. University Press.

Peck, J., & Tickell, A. (2002). A neoliberalizing space. *Antipode, 34*(3), 380–404. https://doi.org/10.1111/1467-8330.00247

Peck, J., & Whiteside, H. (2016). Financializing Detroit. *Economic Geography, 92*(3), 235–268. https://doi.org/10.1080/00130095.2015.1116369

Pike, A. (2023). *Financialization and local statecraft*. Oxford University Press—United Kingdom.

Pike, A., O'Brien, P., Strickland, T., & Tomaney, J. (2019). *Financialising city statecraft and infrastructure*. Edward Elgar.

Rodríguez-Pose, A., & Gill, N. (2003). The global trend towards devolution and its implications. *Environment and Planning C: Government and Policy, 21*(3), 333–351. https://doi.org/10.1068/c0235

Sandford, M. (2020) *Local government: Commercial property investments*. Research Briefing. House of Commons Library.

Smith, P. (2007). *Formula funding of public services*. Routledge.

Tapp, R., & Kay, K. (2019). Fiscal geographies: "Placing" taxation in urban geography. *Urban Geography, 40*(4), 573–581. https://doi.org/10.1080/02723638.2019.1585141

Tiebout, C. (1956). A pure theory of local expenditures. *Journal of Political Economy, 64*(5), 416–424. https://doi.org/10.1086/257839

Weber, R. (2010). Selling city futures: The financialisation of urban redevelopment policy. *Economic Geography, 86*(3), 251–274. https://doi.org/10.1111/j.1944-8287.2010.01077.x

Werner, J. (2018). *Equalisation among the states in Germany: The junction between solidarity and subsidiarity*. Feda.

4

Local Government in England

Historically, English local government was established on an ad hoc basis in response to specific service needs and local particularism. A range of single purpose bodies developed during the nineteenth century in response to the social conditions created by industrialisation, and between 1888 and 1925 these gradually developed into multi-purpose local authorities (Keith-Lucas & Richards, 1978; Wilson & Game, 2011). The UK has no written constitution, and local government has always occupied a constitutionally subordinate position. Its functions are determined by the UK Parliament; it has no written or conventional rights to particular functions, or funding sources. Its influence in UK public life waxed at the time of the welfare state in the mid-twentieth century, when public sector functions were expansive; at other times, it has been disregarded or engaged in open struggle with central government. For the most part, the UK state has shown little interest in developing a narrative of a clear role for the sector or a coherent approach to central–local relations, instead largely muddling through in response to ephemeral policy requirements.

The mid-twentieth century was a time of exception to the general rule of regarding local government as a second-order concern. In 1974, a

K. Muldoon-Smith et al., *Embedded Autonomy*,
https://doi.org/10.1007/978-981-97-9030-2_4

symmetrical two-tier system of local government was created across all of England. All areas had both a county council and a district council. The intention was for counties to be responsible for large-scale public services (such as education, social care, or transport), while district councils would hold responsibility for matters such as housing, environment, or waste. The division of functions was slightly different in six metropolitan counties (established in England's largest conurbations) and Greater London. Table 4.1 shows the standard division of functions between the two tiers, which has changed only marginally since 1974.

Table 4.1 Division of functions in two-tier system

Function	Tier
Arts and recreation	County/district
Births, deaths, and marriage registration	County
Building regulations	District
Burials and cremations	District
Children's services	County
Coastal protection	District
Community safety	District
Concessionary travel	County
Consumer protection	County
Council tax and business rates	District
Economic development	County/district
Education, including special educational needs, adult education, pre-school	County
Elections and electoral registration	District
Emergency planning	County
Environmental health	District
Highways (not trunk roads), street lighting, and traffic management	County
Housing	District
Libraries	County
Licensing	District
Markets and fairs	District
Minerals and waste planning	County
Museums and galleries	County/district
Parking	County/district
Passenger transport (buses) and transport planning	County
Planning	County/district
Public conveniences	District

(*continued*)

Table 4.1 (continued)

Function	Tier
Public health	County
Social services, including care for the elderly and community care	County
Sports centres, parks, playing fields	District
Street cleaning	District
Tourism	County/district
Trading standards	County
Waste collection and recycling	District
Waste disposal	County

Source: Sandford (2022) Local Government in England: Structures

Local authorities in England exercise functions assigned to them by Parliament. Many of those functions are augmented by detailed statutory duties in numerous different Acts of Parliament.

Since 1972, the number of local authorities in England has fallen. The metropolitan county councils have been abolished and their functions passed to district councils in their areas. In other cases, district councils in large cities have obtained county-level powers; in others, councils had been merged into single units. Most of the changes have been symptomatic of the UK government's reflex preference for a single tier of local government.

The Local Government Association is the representative membership body covering almost all local authorities in England. However, England has no formal standing intergovernmental structures through which negotiation can take place. Consultation on policy matters is ad hoc and takes place at central government discretion. Likewise, the UK has no written constitution and there is no concept of constitutional protection or 'constitutional statutes' that serve to protect local government's status or interests.

In the two-tier parts of England, there are 21 county councils (upper tier) and 164 district councils (lower tier), each county contains several districts. Responsibility for services is split between the two tiers in these areas. In other areas, a single 'unitary authority' takes on the responsibilities of both tiers. These come in slightly different forms: 63 unitary

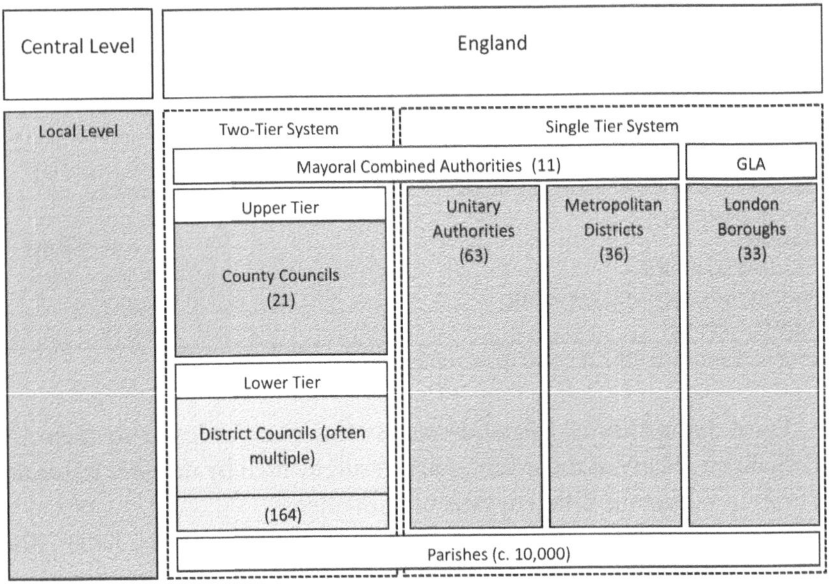

Fig. 4.1 Subnational governance structure in England

authorities, 36 metropolitan districts, and 33 London boroughs.[1] Figure 4.1 describes this situation in England.

There is a further tier of around 10,000 parish and town councils in some parts of England. These are the smallest tier of governance, covering 91% of the geography of England but only around 36% of the population. They have minimal funding and powers. They do not correspond with, and should not be compared to, municipal governments in other states that cover small geographical areas or populations. At the time of writing, there are eleven mayoral combined authorities and the Greater London Authority, which exercise certain strategic functions. Some of these cover the same areas as the 1974 metropolitan counties.

Local authority councillors are elected every four years. Some are elected on a rolling basis, with one-third of councillors elected each year and a 'fallow' fourth year. Others are elected at four-yearly elections. The

[1] These figures include the City of London and the Isles of Scilly, which have unique governance structures for historical and geographical reasons. Their financial arrangements are unique and cannot be easily compared to other local authorities.

public has no right to recall councillors or mayors during their terms of office. Councillors have no power to express no confidence in a mayor or a fellow councillor, or to expel them for misdemeanours. Similarly, though the central government has substantial powers to intervene in local authorities, it cannot dissolve councils and order early elections. It also has no legal obligation to assist councils that encounter financial difficulties.

Some local government services are statutory: Parliament has created a legal duty for councils to provide them. Many of these are subject to statutory requirements or guidance, or provisions derived from case law, and they will often be subject to national inspection or monitoring regimes. They can be distinguished from mandatory services: these are services which local authorities only have a general duty to provide, but to avoid legal challenges they must be provided to a certain standard in practice. Discretionary services are services that local authorities may choose to provide: these include leisure centres, street lighting, recreation grounds, or public toilets. The distinction between statutory, mandatory, and discretionary services does not equate to the distinction found in some states between local functions and 'agency functions' carried out by local authorities on behalf of the government.[2] Some responsibilities are known as 'concurrent' and can be undertaken by either tier of government.

These different types of function are not reflected in finance arrangements for local authorities. There are no distinct funding arrangements for statutory and mandatory functions and for discretionary functions. Where ring-fenced funding is provided, this is largely for historical reasons, for instance:

- Single-purpose fire and rescue authorities and Police and Crime Commissioners receive direct funding from central government.
- Local authorities must pass school education funding directly to schools.
- Local authorities administer housing benefits in accordance with national entitlements.
- Public health funding, which was transferred to local authorities in 2013, is ring-fenced.

[2] See David Wilson and Chris Game, Local Government in the United Kingdom, 5th edition, 2011.

- Councils that provide council housing must ring-fence the proceeds of asset sales, rental income, and spending on maintenance in a separate 'housing revenue account'.
- The National Health Service operates entirely independently of local authorities. A small amount of funding is provided to the NHS for joint use with local authority partners.
- Ring-fencing of funding for local government functions is rare. The UK Government sometimes provides grant programmes intended for use on specific purposes but without insisting on authorities using it for that purpose. These have been referred to as 'visible lines of funding'.

Local Government Finance Policy in England

The UK government is responsible for local government finance policy in England. Allocations of central transfer grants, and some redistribution of business rates revenue, are fixed through an annual funding round (the 'local government finance settlement'), determined between November and February before the beginning of the UK financial year in April. The distribution of these funds is entirely in the hands of the UK government. These are supplemented by a small group of conditional grants. The remainder of local authority income comes principally from property taxes: council tax (domestic property) and business rates (non-domestic property), together with more minor contributions from local fees and charges and investment income.

The Regulatory Regime

Local authorities must produce an annual budget, by specified dates. This must include details of their forecast income for the following financial year, including any funds taken from or transferred into their reserves. It must also specify the amount to be raised from council tax (domestic property taxation). There is no central supervision of the budget process, nor does central government have any sanctioning powers if a budget is not passed.

There is no requirement for the budget to be inspected or signed off by the Government or any independent body. The local authority's Chief Finance Officer must report to the council on the robustness of estimates made and the state of financial reserves assumed in budget calculations. If there is or is likely to be unlawful expenditure or an unbalanced budget, the Chief Finance Officer is under a statutory obligation to issue a report. The Council then is required to meet within 21 days to discuss and rectify this situation.

Four statutory codes of practice regulate local authority financial management. These cover:

- Treasury management.
- Investment guidance (how the council makes decisions about which financial institutions and assets it invests or deposits funds with).
- Minimum revenue provision (the amount to be set aside annually to repay borrowing).
- Borrowing (the Prudential Code).

These statutory codes form core 'institutional logics' within English local government, and influence 'material practices' decisively (Ferry & Eckersley, 2020). These codes have the status of statutory guidance. Local authorities must publish a strategy document for each, which must 'have regard' to the guidance. This approach permits them to deviate from the statutory code providing that they explain why they are doing so. There is also no regulatory body tasked with ensuring that local authorities follow the codes, nor do statutory sanctions exist for local authorities or officials that fail to do so.

Local authorities must undergo annual external audits. These are collectively commissioned by local authorities from private sector audit firms. They must include an opinion on the council's arrangements for securing economy, efficiency, and effectiveness in resource use. The auditors have the right to investigate individual items of spending, to declare spending unlawful, and to apply to a court for a declaration if an item in the accounts is unlawful or to prevent unlawful spending. These legal rights are used very rarely. Section 3 of the Accounts and Audit Regulations 2015 requires the council to have a sound system of internal control to ensure that financial and operational management is effective. Controls are documented in a council's Financial Regulations. Every council is legally required to publish annual financial statements that follow a standardised format set by CIPFA's Code of Governance and Audit.

The flexibility available in financial management, and the lack of any monitoring authority (Eckersley, 2024),[3] has encouraged some English local authorities to pursue unorthodox practices. These have risen in profile following financial pressures emanating from reductions in transfer grants since 2010 (see below). For instance, some have transferred sums from their capital to their revenue accounts. This must normally only be done for specific purposes and in line with a published strategy, but some local authorities have not followed that requirement. This practice has been discovered through post-hoc Government intervention in authorities that have suffered financial or service failures: that is, after the event. In contrast to the international locations in this book, the English local government finance system does not have a systematic or proactive monitoring regime. Rather, local governments are largely required to self-report their practice within a system of guidance.

Capital Finance

The English system requires local authorities to clearly distinguish between revenue and capital spending. Capital spending is "spending to purchase or improve physical assets that may depreciate in value over time, such as property or infrastructure (land, buildings, rail, road, utilities)" (Muldoon-Smith & Sandford, 2021). Capital funds cannot be used to fill gaps in revenue spending: they must be kept separate. This also applies to 'capital receipts'—funds obtained by selling properties or assets. However, revenue funding can be transferred to capital funds. Local authorities may borrow only for capital investments, not revenue spending.

[3] The Audit Commission used to provide this oversight, but local public audit was essentially privatised after this body was abolished in 2015. The outgoing conservative government recognised this had become a problem and accepted (though did not implement) the findings of the 2020 Redmond Review that sought to address the problem.

Capital spending can be funded in two ways: funding it upfront or financing it over time using borrowing. Upfront funding can come from various sources, such as government grants, the sale of capital assets, and revenue income. Borrowing can be sourced internally from areas such as temporary surplus cash holdings or externally from the Public Works Loan Board, commercial banks, or other local authorities. Local authorities can also issue bonds, alone or via the Municipal Bonds Agency.

It is very rare for local authorities to invest in joint projects with private or other public sector partners. Infrastructure projects that are constituted as a partnership with central government (and which therefore have joint funding arrangements) are almost unknown.[4]

According to National Statistics, in 2023–2024, total capital spending was £29.6 billion (1% higher than the previous year). Capital grants were the largest financing source for capital expenditure at £12.5 billion, making up 43% of total resources used to finance capital expenditure. Prudential borrowing accounted for £10 billion (34%), followed by revenue resources at £4.7 billion (16%) and capital receipts at £2.2 billion (7%) (DLUHC, 2024a). Housing and highways accounted for the majority of expenditure in 2023–2024, while total capital expenditure is forecast to increase to £30.9 billion in the year 2024–2025, a 5% increase (DLUHC, 2024a). The majority of local authority borrowing comes from the Public Works Loan Board (PWLB), which typically can offer interest rates close to sovereign debt levels. Local borrowing is largely self-regulated within a system of underlying legislation complemented by the Prudential Code. This allows local authorities to borrow funds within borrowing limits that they set themselves. The Government does not place a cap on individual or total borrowing levels and does not need to approve borrowing in advance. There is no limit on local authority borrowing related to the local authority's income or its income from local sources (as is commonly found in private or commercial financing and local government finance practice in Europe). In the wake of a small number of local authorities experiencing severe financial difficulties in the early 2020s, the Government has tightened legal powers to cap borrowing levels and to direct local authorities to dispose of specific assets under certain circumstances.

---

[4] The Crossrail project in London is a very large and high-profile exception to this rule.

Sources of Income

In general, councils have access to four main revenue sources: council tax, the settlement funding assessment (including locally retained business rates and the revenue support grant), other central government grants, and sales, fees, and charges. These funding sources are not ring-fenced: their revenue forms one single spending fund. The sources of local government spending power can be seen below in order of their overall contribution.

Council tax is a tax on domestic property set by local authorities, which retain its revenue. Annual increases are subject to central caps, which can traditionally only be overruled through a local referendum. In 2022–2023, council tax accounted for 19% of total local authority income (DLUHC, 2024b). The Government has instituted minor extensions to the council tax system since 2010, principally to permit higher charges on second homes and empty properties.

Business rates are a tax on non-domestic property. In 2022–23, business rates accounted for 8% of local authority income (DLUHC, 2024a). Since 2013–2014, under the business rate retention scheme (BRRS), local authorities have been able to retain 50% of business rate income. Local authorities have no control over the valuation of properties for business rates purposes (the rateable value is set by the National Valuation Office Agency) and cannot alter the national tax rate in the form of the national multiplier.[5] Mandatory reliefs are set by the UK Government, while billing authorities can grant additional discretionary relief. A small number of areas (Greater Manchester, Liverpool City Region, West Midlands, West of England, and Cornwall) have piloted the retention of 100% of business rates growth, while forgoing some grant revenue.

Transfer grants accounted for 46% of local authority income in 2022–2023. This represented some £89,537 billion in 2022–2023, down from £94,653 billion the previous year: this steep change comprises the

[5] Some councils can establish a supplementary multiplier (a business rate supplement), which is subject to a confirmatory referendum of rate-paying businesses. Only one supplement has ever been established. Authorities may also establish business improvement districts, at the demand of local businesses, which can charge a supplementary multiplier in a defined locality, either on all businesses or businesses in a specific sector.

tapering away of additional Covid-19 funding (DLUHC, 2024a). In addition, local authority reserves also play a significant role in the system and are often used to make up the shortfall between income and expenditure to balance budgets.

Fees and charges are largely set by central government at levels that reflect the cost of providing the service for which they are charged. Since 2011, English local authorities have also had broader powers to operate discretionary services on a commercial basis. Initiatives include providing training services, establishing trading companies, providing loans to third parties at commercial rates, and undertaking joint ventures with private developers. Some have borrowed substantial sums of money to invest in commercial property, which is then rented out, and the profits invested in local services. In 2022–2023, income from sales, fees, and charges totalled £15.1 billion, equivalent to 8% of total income (DLUHC, 2024a).

Forms of Land Value Capture are also used. The most common form is "Section 106 agreements" between developers and local authorities, where developers provide benefits (normally in kind, such as roads or other infrastructure) as part of planning permission requirements. The cash value of section 106 agreements is not regularly recorded but was estimated at £5 billion per year in 2016–2017 (MHCLG, 2017). Local authorities have also been able to establish a Community Infrastructure Levy (CIL) on new commercial floor space. CIL generated £375 million in England in 2021–2022. These funds must be spent on 'infrastructure' and cannot be repurposed to supplement public service spending. Other small-scale forms of land value uplift are used, such as Tax Increment Finance districts (currently known as Accelerated Development Zones) to repay the borrowed cost of development property value uplift (e.g., in Newcastle-upon-Tyne). Local authorities also have the power to introduce road pricing schemes and a levy on workplace parking. A number of local authorities introduced small road pricing zones in the early 2020s, normally to improve air quality (for instance, 'Clean Air Zones' or 'Zero Emissions Zones').

In summary, due to the characteristics of the local government finance system, English local authorities have little control over the tax rates of their major sources of local revenue. This reduces the incentive for them to take action that would increase the tax revenue from those sources:

there are few options available to them. Levies such as road pricing or CIL generate smaller amounts of revenue and cannot substitute for property taxes or for large reductions in transfer grant funding.

Degree of Own Ubdgeting and Accounting

In 2022–2023, English local authorities spent £111,330 million of revenue funding in support of public services. Spending was dominated by statutory services, with education accounting for 33% of revenue expenditure and adult and children's social care accounting for 30%. In comparison, cultural, planning, and environmental services only accounted for 9% of revenue expenditure—a contrast indicating the pressures on discretionary spending since 2010. Table 4.2 describes the various local government income sources in comparative and percentage format. While the table indicates that grant and local income contribute broadly

Table 4.2 Summary of local authority income 2022–2023

Revenue Type	% of income
Transfer Grants	
Revenue Support Grant	1%
Police Grant	4.4%
Specific and special grants inside Aggregate External Finance (AEF)	26.6%
Local Services Support Grant (LSSG)	0%
Grants outside AEF	7.8%
Housing Revenue Account Government Grants and Assistance	0%
Grants towards capital expenditure	5.9%
Taxes (shared and local)	
Council tax	18.6%
Retained Income from Rate Retention Scheme	8.4%
Charges and Income	
External interest receipts	1.3%
Capital receipts	2.3%
Sales, fees, and charges	7.7%
Council rents	3.9%
Other income and adjustments	12%
Total Revenue	100%

Source: Local Government Financial Statistics England (2024b)

similar amounts, local authorities have very little control over the generation, alteration, and use of the local income. Nor is there a clear relationship between central grants and local needs.

The English system has no shared framework within which local and central government can negotiate new responsibilities and assess the funding required to deliver them. There is no provision in statute for how the amounts, and distribution, of transfer grants should be calculated. This means that there are no legal or formal means for local authorities to challenge the amount of transfer grant funding they receive, as it is given entirely at the discretion of the Government and largely without formal parameters or a shared process of negotiation between state and local government. This system also lacks any incentive or mechanism for local and central government to work in mutually beneficial partnership to tackle the dynamic issues impacting local areas.

This lack of control over funding has been accompanied, since 2010, by severe reductions in transfer grants—principally the general-purpose Revenue Support Grant, which has fallen from £15 billion in 2013–2014 to some £2 billion in 2022–2023. Analysis from the Institute for Government (2020) states central government grants were cut by 37% between 2009–2010 and 2019–2020. These funding cuts have been sufficiently large that local governments have been unable to replace them with local income sources—the overall spending power of local government reduced by at least 50% between 2010–2011 and 2020–2021 alone (National Audit Office, 2021).

Historically, an informal understanding existed that the UK Parliament should provide local authorities with the funding required to undertake responsibilities that Parliament itself had imposed on local authorities (Sandford, 2016). However, this understanding has withered since the early 2010s: functions and needs have become uncoupled from financial provision. The opacity of grant funding formulae and practices is such that the concept of 'unfunded mandates'—local authorities being required to undertake tasks that they lack the funding to do effectively—barely emerges in the English debate.

The ensuing financial pressure has incentivised local authorities to seek new sources of revenue. Two principal sources have been pursued in recent years. One is competitive funding, in the form of central government funds for short-term projects. Funding available through this source has totalled several billion pounds per year in recent years. Another is the use of borrowing and capital spending to generate commercial revenue.

Method of Territorial Equalisation

Historically, English local authority grant funding was distributed according to a complex process of needs and resource assessment. This operated between 1959 and 2013 and used various methodologies. In each case, multiple indicators relating to the core functions of local authorities (for instance, housing and homelessness; environmental services; waste; planning and regulatory services adult social care; children and young people's services; public health; highways maintenance) were assigned a weighting, leading to an allocation of funding in respect of each service area. Local authorities' capacity to collect council tax was also considered, as was population.

This needs assessment varied in approach over time and was given varying names. For instance, between 2007 and 2013, it was known as the "Relative Needs Formula", and from 1990 to 2007 as the "Standard Spending Assessment". The needs assessment was re-run each year, and allocations of the Revenue Support Grant were based on the outcomes.

Since 2012–2013, no needs assessment has been operated. This was a deliberate choice: the intention was for local authority revenues to be driven more strongly by the retention of growth in business rates revenue—thus incentivising the growth of local businesses and related economies within local authority boundaries. Regular needs assessments could have led to changes in grant allocations that cancelled out some or all of the effect of changes in business rate revenues. Business rate revenue is still redistributed between local authorities, but this is based on the 2012–2013 needs assessment, which has in effect been frozen. Business rate retention was intended to be subject to regular 'resets', where the 'frozen' needs assessment from 2012–2013 is updated. However, the first reset is not now expected to take place before 2026.

The effect of the 2013 needs assessment is therefore increasingly residual—in part because the Revenue Support Grant has been reduced substantially since 2013, and in part because of additional grants that emerged in the late 2010s. These have often been distributed according to specific criteria that relate to only one element of need. For instance, a Rural Services Delivery Grant of £85 million per year has been distributed since 2016–2017 to local authorities according to measures of sparsity.

Summary of the Current Situation

Despite some powers being transferred to localities via a series of devolution deals, the 'Whitehall knows best' model continues to dominate the English system. In the domain of local government finance, the current system has recently been described as a "bidding and begging bowl culture" by the former Conservative Mayor of the West Midlands, Andy Street. That is, the nature of the local government finance system enables a situation where central government continues to control the purse-strings of local authorities. Local authorities have few means of raising revenues of their own. As a result, they depend on funding from central government to provide public services due to their inability to finance these services independently.

This dependence provides food for thought in the light of rhetoric in recent years in favour of autonomy for local government, indicating that while local authorities have more liability for funding various demands, they are operating in a system that does not support the financing of these requirements in terms of quantum, nor does it aim to guarantee certainty in the medium to long term. In addition, while central government has moved away from needs-based funding in favour of apparent local autonomy, in comparison to other countries it has not meaningfully embedded autonomy into a comprehensive system of financing, support, and monitoring of local authorities' activities. In short, local government in England is largely untethered within a system of superficial autonomy. There is very little link between local revenues and decision making apart from the margins of local government activity.[6] Local authorities do not have the power, or the underpinning finance and certainty, to exert their own intentions or to adapt and evolve in response to changes in respective local authority environments. Compared with pre-2013, it can even be contended that local government has less power and room to innovate as the burden of local needs has increased.

This contention can be placed in the wider context of long-standing practitioner discontent with funding and finance policy, from the English local government sector itself. The main sources of this discontent can be summarised as:

- Severe reductions in central transfer grants for English local government since 2010. In parallel, a longer-term shared understanding that central government should pay for local authorities to undertake statutory duties required by Parliament has disappeared.
- Successive rounds of competitive funding and short-term funding settlements that leave little room for medium to long-term planning. Considerable sums of money are distributed via competitive bid processes with little consideration of actual local place-based objectives. This also creates a bureaucratic overhead (in terms of cost and time) for local authorities with no guarantee of success. The absence of constitutional protection and the range of central government discretion over funding disincentivises local authorities from long-term planning. Grant funding is normally provided on an annual basis, and no longer-term structure has existed in recent years. The absence of agreed data on need for local government services, or a framework in which to address that need, means that conversations about 'unfunded mandates' cannot even begin. This creates a situation where local government is not able to adapt quickly to changing local circumstances, rather it must wait for instruction and resource from central government.
- There is marginal control over local revenue. Local authorities have little scope in practice to increase revenue from the two nominally

[6] E.g., new business rates or community infrastructure levy contributions associated with new developments.

local property taxes, council tax, and business rates. Several other local revenues are available, but the levels of income are peripheral in most locations. Examples include transport levies, the Community Infrastructure Levy, and increased council tax on empty and second homes. The Government has shown little inclination to consider new forms of local taxation.

- The result is that reductions in transfer grants since 2010 have incentivised increases in local tax revenues to only a limited degree. This is because English local authorities lack control over the core levers of the property-related council tax and business rates system. In addition, the buoyancy of property markets across locations is not uniform, with some locations far more lucrative and responsive to policy initiatives than others. Consequently, there is very little redundancy in the English local government finance system. If one of the few local income sources fails or is disrupted, there is very little alternative resource to step in and maintain system performance. Instead, the local government finance system is brittle and rigid and prone to failure because it cannot self-organise and evolve in the short, medium, or long term.
- Since 2016, an indefinite pause for the 'Fair Funding Review', which was a review of the needs and resource assessment underlying part of the central transfer grant system. This has implications for the relative funding levels for local authorities in more and less deprived areas of England. The lack of movement on this point contributes to local support for local autonomy, as trust in central government has eroded. This situation is exacerbated by the continued absence of a meaningful and well-resourced vehicle for local-state dialogue and negotiation.
- The struggle for funding resulting from reductions in transfer grants has incentivised English local authorities to seek additional revenues from the capital finance system. In international terms, this system is relatively unregulated. Some English authorities have been able to generate considerable commercial revenues and bolster their finances, while others have been criticised for suspect investment practices. The absence of a general-purpose financial regulator and a struggling audit system for local government also catalysed this practice.

- There is recognition that locations have distinctive characteristics and development pathways that require place-based approaches. The lack of assigned national taxes present in other countries—for instance, income tax, corporation tax, or capital gains tax—disincentivises local authorities from investing in their places. The advantages of connecting tax revenues with policy in this way were noted by the 2009 Calman Commission, which laid the ground for the current fiscal devolution structures in Scotland. The result is very little scope for local authorities to explore and develop new patterns of behaviour on their own terms, precluding adaptation and innovation. The notions of shared taxes and shared endeavour have developed little traction in England.
- Reductions in transfer grants, and hence in budgets, have incentivised local authorities to protect statutory services—as they are open to legal challenge if they do not do so. Many discretionary services have been reduced substantially, and disproportionality in coverage, as a result.
- The regulatory system for English local government is largely law-based. This disincentivises regular, formal, central–local relations. This has consequences that appear contradictory at first glance. For instance, local authorities in financial difficulties in England cannot expect direct central government support; but central government also shies away from financial oversight. This calls to mind Bulpitt's 'central autonomy thesis' (1983), that central government's core aim is to avoid responsibility for the actions of lower tiers of government, not to control those actions. In other words, central government does not micromanage local government, rather it drip-feeds resource in a detached and largely unobserved manner. While this creates the conditions for a certain degree of apparent compliance, centralised disinterest has created a local government system that throttles autonomy rather than embedding it.

The initial chapters in the book have set out the case for investigating local government finance, both as an immediate issue of concern in England but also for the international local government finance system as it struggles to fund and govern the multiple challenges. We have also argued for system thinking and the importance of using local government finances as a meaningful lens for understanding territorial development before setting out how local government finance currently works in

England. The next three chapters will examine practice in the three case study locations—Germany, Italy, and Japan—as a means of considering how practice and reform could take place in England.

References

Bulpitt, J. (1983). *Territory and power in the United Kingdom*. Manchester University Press.

DLUHC. (2024a). *Local authority capital expenditure and receipts in England: 2023 to 2024 final outturn*.

DLUHC. (2024b). *Local government financial statistics England no.34 2024*. UK Government.

Eckersley, P. (2024). Financial precarity in English local government. *IPPR Progressive Review, 31*(2), 89–94. https://doi.org/10.1111/newe.12393

Ferry, L., & Eckersley, P. (2020). Hybridizing the institutional logics of performance improvement and budgetary stewardship in English and Welsh local government. *Public Policy and Administration, 35*(1), 45–64. https://doi.org/10.1177/0952076718781433

Institute for Government. (2020). *Local government funding in England*. Institute for Government.

Keith-Lucas, B., & Richards, P. G. (1978). *A history of local government in the twentieth century*. Routledge.

MHCLG. (2017). *A new approach to developer contributions*. UK Government.

Muldoon-Smith, K., & Sandford, M. (2021). Grasping the nettle: The central–local constraints on local government funding in England. *Territory, Politics, Governance, 1-18*. https://doi.org/10.1080/21622671.2021.1924249

National Audit Office. (2021). *The local government finance system in England: Overview and challenges*. National Audit Office.

Redmond Review. (2020). *Independent review into the oversight of local audit and the transparency of local authority financial reporting*.

Sandford, M. (2016). Public services and local government: The end of the principle of funding following duties. *Local Government Studies, 42*(4), 637–656. https://doi.org/10.1080/03003930.2016.1171753

Sandford, M. (2022). *Local government in England: Structures*. House of Commons Library.

Wilson, D., & Game, C. (2011). *Local government in the United Kingdom* (5th ed.). Palgrave Macmillan.

5

Local Government in Germany

Introduction: Political Economy in Germany

Like England, German local government relies heavily on local taxes, particularly property-related income streams and trade tax. German local government also benefits from shared proportions of income tax and VAT to fund services and infrastructure demands. Even with these financial levers, there is still widespread consensus that local income alone is not sufficient to cover local costs, leading to budget deficits and constrained decision making. Consequently, despite a relative degree of autonomy, German municipalities still rely on intergovernmental transfers to fund relative spending need. Economic fluctuations or any change in financial policy can impact on this type of revenue. Fluctuation is typically counter-cyclical with more transfer during recession or emergency. This results in demand for proactive intergovernmental fiscal relations to ensure place-based objectives are achieved.

Local government financial resilience in Germany is strongly correlated with the regional and local economies (due to its reliance on local business tax) while the Länder are more reliant on the national economy due to their reliance on shared VAT. While fiscal equalisation measures

K. Muldoon-Smith et al., *Embedded Autonomy*,
https://doi.org/10.1007/978-981-97-9030-2_5

exist in Germany, both horizontally and increasingly vertically, significant inequality and uneven development still exists. This has some parallels with the north-south divide in England—particularly in those locations with less economic resource and underlying property market-based rental conditions. This inequality is particularly evident in those locations that have suffered from deindustrialisation.

There is also a sharp contrast between the former East and West Germany, with greater financial support from state government in place in former East German locations. Generally, local government has been reducing its debt burden and improving its financial position following constitutional changes in relation to appropriate debt and balanced budgets. In some locations this 'debt brake' has led to austerity measures that have constrained investment. Covid-19 demanded the suspension of so-called 'debt brake' rules with subnational government temporarily allowed to operate with unbalanced budgets. More recently, the constitutional court in Germany has also questioned the accountancy manoeuvres that have been used to circumvent the 'debt brake' and this has led to a gap in the public finances with some questioning the rigidity of the brake.

Subnational Governance Structure in Germany

The German federal system of government is grounded in the 1949 Basic Law (Grundgesetz für die Bundesrepublik Deutschland) and is based on the principle of co-operative federalism (Bundestreue). The federal state (Bund) is a three-tiered system of subnational governance: 16 Länder (regions or states), 400 Kreise (districts), and 10,786 Stadt and Gemeinden (municipalities).[1] The subnational governance structure is displayed in Fig. 5.1.

Below the Länder (state) are the Kreise (counties) which are divided into 294 rural districts (Landkreise) and 106 urban districts/independent cities (Stadtkreise—akin to urban unitary authorities in England). The majority of German districts are Landkreise, which occupy an

[1] Berlin, Hamburg and Bremen are city states and have different local government structures. The figure of 106 Stadtkreise includes Berlin, Hamburg, Bremen, and Bremerhaven.

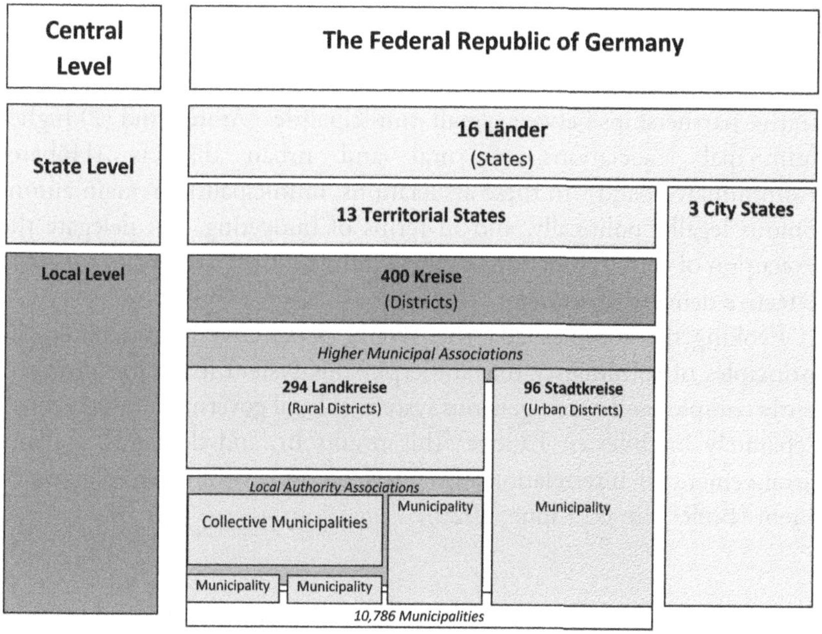

Fig. 5.1 Subnational governance structure of Germany

intermediate level of administration to act as the primary subdivision between state and local level for a group of municipalities. The remaining are Stadtkreise (106), which are single municipalities that have administrative autonomy over a designated urban area and combine the administrative functions of local and district level. The Landkreise are then divided into collective municipalities and single municipalities which may be Städte (cities) or Gemeinden (town/community).

The Municipal Code in Germany (Gemeindeordnung) supports local authority associations between municipalities. This can be on a voluntary basis at the regional or local level (known as Gemeindeverbände or Landkreisverbände) in order to coordinate information exchange, joint planning, and the implementation of shared projects; Inter-Municipal Cooperation Agreements (Kooperationsvereinbarungen) that define objectives, responsibilities, financial arrangements, and decision-making processes between participating municipalities; or joint administrative units (Zweckverbände or Kommunalverbände) to coordinate infrastructure and regional planning. In some states, there exist two forms of local authority association between municipalities and districts: (1) administrative partnerships between small municipalities (Ämte), and (2) higher municipal associations of rural and urban districts (Höherer Kommunalverband). In these associations, municipalities remain autonomous legally, politically, and in terms of budgeting, but delegate the execution of certain functions to the administrative partnership for more effective delivery of services.

Evoking the complex adaptive system perspective in this book, the principles of subsidiarity that underpin this system make for an inherently complex and heterogeneous system of local government that evolves separately in different Länder. This results in, and demands, a dense arrangement of interrelationships between and within tiers of government (Bullerjahn & Thöne, 2020).

Responsibilities (Shared and Exclusive)

The Federal Republic of Germany is governed by the rule of law in which the principle of the separation of powers applies. The vertical distribution of power follows the principle of subsidiarity in parallel to the principle of adequate financing at the lowest levels of government. Adequate financing is enshrined in the complementary principles of connexity, equivalence, solidarity, equivalence of living conditions, and loyalty to the Bund (Bullerjahn & Thöne, 2020). Of particular importance for the financial position of local government is 'connexity', which insists that centrally imposed tasks must also be aligned with adequate central funding, and 'equivalence' which insists that revenues must be in symmetry with local services.

The Bund is obliged to assist the lower scale Länder, districts and local authorities in carrying out tasks, but is prevented from intervening if the lower scale entity can perform the tasks on their own. This safeguards the power of decision-making at the local level (through a parliament elected by ballot) and plays an important role in local autonomy. Actual autonomy is underpinned by the principles of municipal self-government

(Kommunale Selbstverwaltung)—this is preserved in the German constitution. Within this principle, local authorities have the right to govern their own affairs, including financial matters, as long as they operate within the boundaries of the law.

According to the division of responsibilities in the Basic Law, the power to regulate local government law lies with the Länder. Article 28 stipulates that the constitutional order in each of the Länder and municipalities must conform to the principles of the democratic and social state governed by the rule of law. The Länder is responsible for ensuring the municipalities perform their functions while according the municipalities the right to self-administration, meaning each municipality has a distinct constitutional mandate to manage the affairs of their local community. The consequence is that each Land has its own local government law and structure, and these can sometimes vary considerably from Land to Land. The respective powers and duties of local governments are detailed in the respective Land's municipal laws, explaining the degree of local autonomy and the specific relationship between municipality, Länder, and Bund.

This contrasts with England, where the division of statutory, mandatory, and discretionary responsibility is relatively fixed. Income is rarely in symmetry with the responsibility of local government in England. The financial constitution (Finanzverfassung) of Germany ensures this alignment, enabling mechanisms for revenue sharing between the federal and state governments, including tax-sharing agreements (where certain taxes are collected jointly and distributed among the different levels of government) and intergovernmental grants (these grants aim to ensure the equalisation of financial capacities among the states and support the provision of public services). The explicit nature of these requirements in the Basic Law provides a different context for subnational behaviour, in the sense that these requirements are justiciable. A Land that attempted to enforce an unfunded mandate could expect challenge within the Land's constitutional court. By the same token, a Land might more easily implement an initiative to merge small municipalities or to add/reduce local government functions by using the Basic Law as a reference point.

The provision of services in Germany follows a 'bottom-up' approach, in that tasks must be completed at the lowest level and are only moved to a higher tier of government when the lower level does not have the means to carry out the task. Functions may be divided into two large areas of responsibility: the municipalities' own sphere of responsibility and the transferred sphere of responsibility. Municipalities' own sphere of responsibility relates to their own activities, which are also known as self-government tasks. There are two types of tasks: voluntary tasks, which are at the discretion of the local authority and could include establishing a theatre, museum, sports field, or municipal hall, and mandatory tasks which include local government matters that the municipality must perform, under federal or Land law. Within the framework of self-government, the municipality is obliged to guarantee mandatory tasks, though the manner in which the municipality fulfils this task is autonomous.[2] The most important mandatory tasks are:

- Providing citizens with water, electricity, district heating, and gas.
- Wastewater services and waste removal.
- Planning municipality territory by specifying residential, commercial, and other areas (town planning).
- Construction and maintenance of local roads and green areas, parks, and cemeteries.
- The construction and operation of own sports and social facilities.
- Cultural and educational work, including the construction or maintenance of own and the promotion of private cultural and educational facilities.
- The construction and operation of hospitals and old people's homes.
- Local public transport.
- The construction and maintenance of schools (although the overall educational framework is held at state level).
- Matters concerning the fire brigade.
- Local economic development.

[2] Note that a number of these tasks do not fall under the responsibility of local government in England, e.g., the provision of energy, passport affairs, and water management.

The transferred sphere of responsibility relates to tasks that are administered at the lowest possible level of government (subsidiarity) under supervision from the state. These tasks are administrative and include:

- General security.
- Nationality, registration, passport affairs.
- Social welfare/housing support/services for the elderly and disabled (the funding for these programs is often shared between the local, state, and federal levels).
- Registrar's office and civil status.
- Commercial affairs.
- Construction matters.
- Road traffic.
- Registration of vehicles and vehicle taxation.
- Collection of local taxes and revenues (local governments have the authority to levy and collect certain local taxes, such as property taxes and local trade taxes, to finance their operations and services).
- Water legislation and land cultivation.
- Federal and Land parliamentary elections.
- Protection and maintenance of historical monuments.
- Statistics
- Forestry and fisheries.

These are administrative state tasks that the Bund or Land may transfer to the municipalities. The Land still exerts control through legal and expert supervision with the entitlement to issue instructions under certain conditions.

At the local level, the districts, towns, and municipalities must fulfil particular functions. Local government tasks are divided between the district on the one hand and the municipality on the other, according to the principle that supra-local services beyond the capacity of the municipality are provided by the district or local authority association. The district is only responsible when the task exceeds the capacity of a municipality. For example, the construction and maintenance of a waste disposal facility exceeds the financial means of an individual municipality, therefore the district takes on this task. In this instance, the municipality is ultimately responsible for administering the waste removal service, but the district is obliged to assist.

These functions are reflected in the financial arrangements for individual municipalities, coordinated and monitored by the Lander. There is also an active element of ring-fenced funding (Zweckbindung). Zweckbindung takes various forms, such as earmarked taxes, grants from higher levels of government, or specific revenue sources tied to particular services or programs. The purpose of ring-fenced funding is to guarantee that the allocated funds are used as intended and to prevent their diversion for other purposes. Due to the heterogeneity of sub-national government in Germany, the actual division of responsibilities and parallel design of adequate funding provision can vary considerably. This variation can be seen in the funding of services by general or ring-fenced funding from the Länder. Funding in one state for a given service could be ring-fenced, while in another it is funded by the general block grant from the Land government.

The Regulatory Regime

The financial constitution (Finanzverfassung) is an important aspect of the German constitutional system and is anchored in the Basic Law. It refers to all regulations that affect the public finance system of a state, including the right to levy taxes and other charges to fulfil its responsibilities and functions. The corresponding provisions are in German Basic Law Articles 104 to 108, regulating:

- The financial sovereignty shared between the Federation and the Länder as well as the financial relations between the Federation, the Länder, and the municipalities.
- The distribution of the burden of expenditure.
- Legislative competence in tax matters.
- Tax revenues.
- The responsibilities of the tax administration and fiscal jurisdiction.

Budgetary and fiscal oversight is incorporated in Articles 109 to 115 of the Basic Law and there is an escalating set of instruments to enforce fiscal rules (De Widt, 2017). One of the key laws is the 'debt brake'. The law was enacted in Article 109(3) and Article 115 and constitutes a fiscal rule that is intended to limit borrowing by the federal and state governments to a budget deficit of 0.35% of GDP—it came into effect in 2011 (Rietzler & Truger, 2019). The aim is to ensure long-term sustainable budget development and to prevent excessive borrowing. This is achieved by countercyclical fiscal policy, which collects surplus funds during an economic boom to offset the deficits of a subsequent recession. The mechanism applies a cyclical factor to receipts to adjust for adverse economic conditions; it is a function of the output gap and defined as the ratio of trend GDP to current GDP. The balancing of receipts and expenditure over the medium term 'flattens' economic cycle fluctuations and enables steady expenditure without the need for liquidity borrowing. While the debt brake was initially met with objections and concerns, the law helped reduce Germany's national debt to 59.5% of GDP, below the 60% threshold. In 2012 and 2013, general government net borrowing was close to zero. In 2014, net borrowing was positive and increasing every year to 2019, until the suspension clause was invoked in 2020 for emergency measures during the Covid-19 pandemic.

Some municipalities have even gone on to voluntarily agree additional rules to constrain borrowing (Geissler et al., 2021; Zabler, 2022), using local byelaws (Satzungen) to exceed the debt restrictions already codified in state law. In parallel the Stability Council (Stabilitätsrat), a body comprising the Bund and the respective Lander, was established in 2010 (enshrined in Article 109a of the Basic Law) to oversee and scrutinise the sustainability of public budgets (Spahn, 2016). The main purpose of the Council is to proactively identify emerging financial emergencies at an early stage and to deploy corrective action before problems materialise.

There is no claim to supervision in the federal constitution; however, local governments in every state must adhere to the balanced budget rule. According to Article 61 of the Basic Law, municipalities must plan and manage their budgets in such a way that they can always perform the required tasks. State authorities supervise the local budgets to ensure they remain within state regulation/budgetary frameworks. Every local government is obliged to hand over its budget plan each year to the respective Land, which assess its general sustainability and violation of the balanced budget rule. If the fiscal rules are broken, the oversight bodies will require the local governments to revise their budget: this is a routine procedure.

In essence, there is a positive trade-off and interplay between autonomy and resilience which is played out via the embedded integration of both in the interrelationship between respective municipality and Lander (Bullerjahn & Thöne, 2020). Constitutionally, municipalities are part of the Länder, who monitor local budgets on a legal basis. In this sense, autonomy is limited by the state oversight system that ensures public services without fiscal problems (Zabler, 2020). At the same time, municipalities have constitutionally guaranteed autonomy (Selbstverwaltungsrecht) which allows them discretion within the budgetary process. In theory, supervisory bodies can do whatever is necessary to proportionately enforce fiscal rules (Roesel, 2017). This means that the constitutional courts—one of which exists in each Land—are very important in managing this trade-off and maintaining autonomy at the lowest level. As the state acts as legislator, leading on scrutiny and ultimate budget sign-off, the codified legal protection for municipalities is an important reference point.

While the maximum escalation for Länder would be sending in a state or austerity commissioner to take measures to improve the budgetary situation (e.g., raising taxes or cutting expenditure) of a municipality, in practice this is very rare. Supervisory bodies tend to take an intermediate role to maintain positive working relationships. As part of a local debt relief programme (Starkungspakt Stadtfinanzen), the state of North Rhine-Westphalia did send state commissioners (sometimes referred to as austerity commissioners) into three municipalities (commencing 2013–2017) to manage non-compliance with agreed austerity plans (Zabler, 2021). However, the vast majority of financial disputes between municipality and Lander are mediated through the constitutional courts—with municipalities invoking the principle of adequate financing and connexity for any new objective.

There is a system of auditing sub-national government that runs in parallel with this process, which is conducted by special independent public bodies. Rechnungshofe (Audit Courts) are responsible for auditing the finances of Land governments and ensuring compliance with financial regulations: there is one associated with each state. Kommunale Prüfungsverbände (Municipal Audit Associations) are established by law to audit local government finance and operate at the level of the Länder.

Capital Finance

Like England, Germany has strict rules governing capital and revenue spending, which in turn defines how local governments manage their resources, distinguishing how different income sources can be used. A local authority's capital spending typically relates to money spent on maintaining and investing in land, buildings, infrastructure, and assets. Public investment is increasingly weighted towards the Lander, accounting for 60% of investment in 2024. In comparative terms, Germany has displayed relatively low levels of debt-based capital investment in recent years (Beznoska & Kauder, 2019). There is a conservative tradition in German local government finance, that municipalities will fund capital investment from their own resources when in surplus. In recent years, even during Covid-19, the German local government finance system has run a surplus (more revenue than expenditure). According to the German statistical agency, in 2022 the Länder spent 522 billion euros (a surplus of nearly 11 billion euros), while local government spent 326 billion euros supporting public services (an overall surplus of 2.6 billion). However, there is more demand for capital investment in those locations that have suffered from de-industrialisation or that form part of the former East Germany.

To improve this situation, the federal government has directly intervened by providing financial support. For example, in 2016 the federal state provided a 7 billion euro Municipal Investment Promotion Fund (Kommunal investitions förderungs fonds) in addition to increased funding for Länder and municipalities for urban development and housing.

In addition, those locations that have been impacted by de-industrialisation also receive support for economic transformation.

In the main, capital spending is financed through capital grants from Länder and the federal state, and municipalities' own income, reserves, and borrowing. Länder account for most sub-national debt (81%) and municipalities account for 18%. Sixty-six per cent of Land debt is made up of bonds and 34% of loans, while municipal debt is made up almost entirely of loans (OECD, 2022). However, in some locations there is a perceived conflict between the previously mentioned debt brake and the need to invest. Falling local revenues in some locations has led to increased interest in using debt and capital financing to make up for shortfalls in public investment—typically via municipal loans or via capital markets (e.g., debt loan certificates and bonds). However, due to the parallel concern of consolidating finance, often through austerity plans, local authorities in this position cannot take on additional debt (in contrast to England where there is no formal basis for permitted levels of debt). This leads to perverse behaviour where municipalities with weak economic fundamentals, and inferior infrastructure and services, must increase local tax more than comparatively stronger locations if they wish to pursue capital investment.

Sources of Revenue

In Germany, local government has access to various revenue sources. There are four major sources of municipal income/revenue: local taxes, joint taxes, charges and concessions, and grants and transfers. Local taxes can be divided into impersonal and personal taxes. Impersonal taxes are the foundation of municipal taxation and predominantly comprise local business tax and property tax. Local business/trade tax (Gewerbesteuer) is levied against business profits and accounts. Municipalities set their own tax rate by applying a multiplier (the Hebesatz) to the minimum base rate (3.5%). This tax revenue is shared between the municipality, the state, and the federal government. The actual rate of this tax currently varies between 8.75% to 20.83% for local authorities with at least 80,000 inhabitants (OECD, 2022). Property tax (Grundsteuer) accounts for approximately 10% of municipalities' tax revenue. There are two types of property taxes, Property Tax A (agricultural and forestry land and properties) and Property Tax B (residential and commercial properties). The municipality determines the multiplier for both property taxes (which is combined with properties' assessed value) and this multiplier can vary considerably between municipalities in different states—this is because different states/regions have varying economic contexts which afford flexibility over tax.

These business and property taxes are retained locally, in contrast to business rates and associated business rate retention in England, where only 50% of revenue is retained locally. While English local authorities may determine the rate of council tax they charge by law, they have limited leeway to adjust the rates as they depend substantially on council tax revenue. German property tax is similarly based on the property's assessed value. However, the municipality determines its own multiplier. They enjoy a high degree of autonomy over property tax revenue; however, financial equalisation methods are designed in such a way that municipalities that set comparatively low tax rates are disadvantaged during the distribution of central grants. This is to avoid unfair tax competition and a race to the bottom between locations (Geissler et al., 2021).

In Germany, in 2018 the Federal Constitutional Court declared the system for calculating property tax as unconstitutional due to underlying values being out of date. Germany has been undertaking new assessments of real property values since 1 January 2022 with new values set to take effect in 2025. Up to that point the existing valuations of 1964 (West Germany) and 1935 (East Germany) were used. The reform maintains the three-step system for calculating the real property tax rate but is based upon updated property values. The tax base rate will be set at 0.034 (3.4%) for business property and 0.031 (3.1%) for housing. Municipalities maintain the ability to determine the effective tax rate by setting an additional multiplier, which is multiplied by the base rate, to produce effective rates that vary between local authorities. The same reform will also enable local authorities to place tax on vacant construction land to prevent land banking and catalyse housing supply in cities.

There are then a variety of relatively minor personal taxes levied by municipalities, for example, dog tax, entertainment tax, liquor tax, and secondary residence tax, that supplement the major impersonal taxes. In addition, there are also a wide range of charges and fees for services such as water, wastewater, refuse collection, and landfill and street cleaning. These only cover the cost of the services provided. Concessions are fees paid by public or private network operators to municipalities in return for rights of way to install electricity, gas, and water infrastructure under public roads. This can then be supplemented by borrowing—municipalities are allowed to take out loans since the above-listed income sources are usually not enough to cover all expenditure. Loans may only be taken for investments or investment promotion measures and if no other means of finance is possible.

The system of joint taxation enables revenue sharing between all three levels of government. It entitles municipalities to a share of joint taxes to supplement their revenue based on population size and fiscal capacity, with each municipality securing a proportion of Personal Income Tax (Einkommensteuer), VAT (Umsatzsteuer) while the Lander receive 50% of corporation tax revenue. This shared tax income forms a significant proportion of total local revenue, although municipalities do not have any discretion to vary the rates of shared taxation.[3]

German local government is also still reliant on grants and transfers. Municipalities receive this revenue predominantly from Länder to directly finance specific programmes and services—there is no direct federal grant to local government. Most of these grants are paid in the form of an overall block allocation which local authorities are free to use as they wish. Often the total sum available through these grants will also take the form of fixed shares of revenue from particular taxes. For example, general revenue sharing grants provide support for operational expenses and public services. Specific purpose grants can fund infrastructure, social welfare programs, education, and health care, typically determined by state or federal legislation. Equalisation grants aim to account for disparities between the relative economic position of a given municipality—providing additional financial support to those locations with weaker economic fundamentals.

---

[3] VAT is shared on the basis of a national redistribution while income tax is based on the contribution of the inhabitants in a given location. Corporation tax (Korperschaftsteuer) is distinct from the local business / trade tax (Gewerbesteuer) though the tax base used by both taxes is similar.

Degree of Own Budgeting and Accounting

In contrast to England, Germany has a more structured sub-national governance system. Intergovernmental finances display complex horizontal and vertical interdependence. As such the degree of autonomous budgeting and discretion must be understood in the context of the Länder and the municipalities (OECD, 2022). Sub-national government in Germany is responsible for half of public spending in Germany. Traditionally, the Länder account for most spending (OECD, 2022)—indicating that the spending responsibility of local authorities is lower than many other countries due to the regional role of the Länder. Within the lowest tier of spending municipalities and associations make up the vast majority of spending, in contrast to districts. In recent years, the Länder and respective municipalities have been able to maintain a healthy financial position. While the cost of delivering services has continued to grow due to demographic trends, expenditure has not outstripped revenue with Länder and local authorities continuing to carry significant surpluses even after the Covid-19 pandemic.

However, there is considerable regional and inter-regional variance with a significant number of municipalities in some Lander (Bavaria, Brandenburg, North Rhine-Westphalia, Rhineland-Palatinate, and Schleswig-Holstein) failing to balance budgets in recent years and carrying high levels of short-term debt (Kassenkredite) (Heinelt & Stolzenberg, 2014). In Germany, municipalities can apply for short-term debt to fill budget gaps. However, in some locations this debt is proving persistent and is not being cleared in line with budgetary conventions nor the German debt brake.

These short-term liquidity tools have largely lost their role as a short-term instrument and have become an indicator of fiscal distress (Zabler, 2020, 2021). In response to this situation, several states have established debt relief programmes (Starkungspakt Stadtfinanzen) where local authorities receive financial relief (from the state budget) in return for their own austerity measures which are codified in consolidation contracts (Boettcher et al., 2017; Zabler, 2022). English authorities facing comparable problems have typically sought permission from the UK government to spend capital revenues to fill budget gaps. While there is no formal bankruptcy regulation in Germany, there is an implicit expectation of financial support when local authorities are in distress.[4]

Social care, public services, and education account for most local authority spending in Germany. Health is a notable exception as it is under the purview of the federal government. At the Lander level, public services (26%), education (24%), and social care (22%) accounted for 72% of total spending.[5] At the local government level, social care (34%), education (17%), and economic affairs (14%) account for 75% of total spending. Across all scales of government, the cost of social care is increasing (Färber & Salm, 2015). In terms of total revenue, Länder accounted for 62% of total sub-national revenue while local government accounted for 38%. Tax revenue accounted for 52% of revenue, grants (between Bund and Länder) 33%, and tariffs and fees 9%. At the local government level, grants (from Länder to municipality) represented 47% of revenue, taxes 40%, and tariffs and fees 13%. Municipalities received 15% of total personal income tax and 2% of VAT.

In 2022, personal income tax represented 35% of total tax revenue and 14% of total local revenue with VAT accounting for 22% of total tax revenue and 9% of total revenue. In terms of locally generated income, the local trade tax contributed most, representing 13% of total revenue and 33% of total local tax (it was significantly higher pre-pandemic and is expected to increase again). In parallel to shared Income Tax and VAT, local authorities share some of this income with the federal government (4%) and the Länder (5%) as part of an upward equalisation process. Property tax accounted for 10% of total tax revenue and 4% of total revenue. In comparison to England, there is considerably less reliance on property tax and by extension on the relative buoyancy of local property markets. Finally, fees and charges accounted for 13% of local government funding, while revenue from assets was not a significant part of either Länder or local authority revenue.

[4] There is very little comprehensive research into local authority insolvency and particularly the underpinning legal framework for insolvency—see INSOL International (2022) for an international analysis.

[5] Figures obtained from OECD World Observatory on Subnational Government Finance and Investment—Germany 2022.

Table 5.1 shows clearly that Germany has considerable, and varied, income sources at the lowest level of government. Its authorities also have more discretion than England's to vary respective tax rates—particularly in the case of trade and property. Property-related taxes only account for 4% of total revenue compared with nearly 20% in England. In addition, overriding much of the debate in relation to types of funding and discretion is the sheer buoyancy of local government finance in Germany, where the system as a whole remains in surplus. In addition, there is a clear constitutional symmetry between revenue and expenditure, hard-wired into intergovernmental cooperation between Bund, Länder, and municipal government.

Table 5.1 Revenue breakdown in Germany

Revenue type	% of income
Transfer Grants (from Länder)	
Finance for specific programmes and services	47%
Taxes (Shared and Local)[a]	
Personal Income Tax	14% (35% of total tax revenue)
VAT	9% (22% of total revenue)
Trade Tax	13% (33% of total tax revenue)
Property tax	4% (10% of total tax revenue)
Minor taxes (Dog Tax, Entertainment Tax, Liquor Tax, and Secondary Residence Tax, etc.)	0%
Charges and income	
Charges for water, wastewater, refuse collection and landfill, street cleaning, and various concessions	13%
Income from assets	0%
Other income	0%
Total Revenue	100%

Source: Information based on adjusted numbers from OECD (2022) World Observatory on Subnational Governance and Investment and the German Statistical Agency. The actual spread of revenue is variegated between location because of equalisation and relative local conditions

[a]Transfer Tax (tax on sale of property) and Corporate Tax are not detailed here as they go to the Lander

Method of Territorial Equalisation

Municipal equalisation is designed to ensure adequate financing, in such a way that it allows efficient financing of tasks, enabling meaningful self-government for all municipalities. When considering equalisation and redistribution, the federal states in Germany are obliged by the Basic Law to perform vertical financial equalisation. An amount of funding is taken from the tax revenues of the federal state and distributed among individual local authorities and local authority associations. Equalisation is based within the principle of solidarity, where municipalities have collective responsibility to support one another. This is to enable all local authorities to provide a comparative level of services and investment, irrespective of the underlying financial conditions of the area. According to Bullerjahn and Thöne (2020), traditionally there have been five different approaches to vertical financial equalisation in Germany:

- Quota model—is the most widely adopted. This sets the total amount of financial equalisation funds as a share of the federal state's overall tax revenues. Quota rates establish the share of federal state revenue that is passed to the municipalities.
- Quota model with symmetry requirement—the symmetry requirements add additional elements to consider. These include not only the tax revenue from all the regular revenues from the federal state level and municipal level, but also the burdens resulting from task responsibility at both levels. The distribution of financing is therefore in line with task responsibility, a key difference to the current situation in England.
- Stabilisation model—an extended form of the quota model. The aim is to stabilise municipal finances by balancing the potential fluctuations in overall tax revenues from the federal state. These fluctuations are buffered by a stability fund, making it possible to balance deficits and top-up funds when surpluses are available.
- Principle of uniformity—this runs in parallel to the quota system and considers the revenues at municipal and federal state level. It creates a direct link between finances at the local level and the federal state. If

income grows more strongly at one of these levels, it has a positive impact on the other level.

- Needs-based system—this is geared towards municipal tasks and the expenditure they instigate. Depending on federal state capacity, the minimum financing is topped up. This requires time-consuming and updated data surveys to determine the cost of individual tasks and comparison between expenditure and income.

Traditionally, the principle of horizontal financial equalisation then ensured that the federal state redistributed local authority revenue to individual municipalities according to fiscal needs, derived from financial requirements and fiscal capacity. Historically, the transfer system was designed as a vertical equalisation with a horizontal effect (Bullerjahn & Thöne, 2020)—federal state funds were distributed according to the capacity of the individual municipalities to generate their own income. Revenue-weak municipalities therefore received more formula-based grants and revenue-strong municipalities received few if any grants. This was based upon:

- Fiscal capacity—calculated according to the municipal revenue from joint taxes and the standardised revenue from property tax and local business tax.
- Financial requirements—determining a needs indicator relative to the municipalities' fiscal capacity, while ensuring that all available funding for formula-based central grants and abundance payments is completely used up. The so-called 'basic amount' is calculated in each financial equalisation year as a monetary multiplier. A structural needs assessment (total appropriation) indicates the individual municipality's financial requirements to perform its duties and is multiplied by the basic amount to calculate apportionment. The total appropriation is most obviously determined by population size, which is the central factor for determining requirements and forms the basis of inhabitant weighting.
- Formula-based allocations—given by the state to municipalities within the framework of local authority fiscal equalisation. This was designed to balance the large differences in taxable capacity as well as allowing

central municipalities to bear the burden of providing services for the surrounding area. A municipality received formula-based grants if its requirements are greater than its own fiscal capacity, which was calculated based on income from joint taxes and standardised income from impersonal taxes. This ensured the financially weak municipalities received the most formula-based grant funding.

The current equalisation system continues to evolve. In 2020 there was an alteration to the share of VAT between Bund and Länder, increasing the Länder's share of VAT (an additional 3.6 billion euros) with the weakest regions benefiting most. One element of the horizontal distribution of this money has been discontinued. This means that the strongest Länder will not have to contribute directly into the system to support weaker Länder. Instead, the Bund now supports the weaker regions via additional vertical equalisation measures.

Summary

The following observations can be made about the German local government finance system, as it relates to the potential for change in England.

- Local government finance in Germany is an example of a complex adaptive system that continually evolves to account for regional and local variation and circumstance. Local autonomy is embedded into the German Basic Law. It affords local government the right to self-administration through the principle of republicanism while principles of connexity and financial equivalence are central components of the constitution.
- This means that German local government finance is not specifically autonomous, in the sense that a given local government unit will not act independently of all other local government units and structures. Rather, German local government is an example of what the authors present as embedded autonomy. Autonomy is located within, and supported by, continual system-based intergovernmental cooperation and

interstate relations. Where the system provides resource and certainty for each local government to engage in a degree of autonomous practice. In the German case, the complex and multiple designed interactions in the local government finance system produce a resilience that could not be afforded by only concentrating on an individual component or single local authority. The collective dynamics of the individual parts of the local government system create the conditions for embedded autonomy.

- Any proposed financial changes have a fixed reference point in the German Constitution and associated legislation. In England, changes would typically take place through an Act of Parliament. This introduces a dependence on central government focus, and the local government sector has no way of obstructing a determined government.
- German local government function, and associated finance, is based on subsidiarity and empowered local governments. The methodology for allocating funding is based on a redistribution of tax revenues through actual financial requirements, calculated based on actual revenue and expenditure data. In England the system is based on central framing of organisational structures, with the state allocating responsibility for functions to 'subordinate' levels of government.
- German municipal revenue is more diverse than England with municipalities receiving a higher share of their revenues through tax, particularly local business tax. Municipalities also receive shares of income tax and VAT. In contrast, the English system is grounded upon grants from central government and an overriding reliance on an increasingly restricted property tax. The reliance on property tax presents a risk as property markets become more volatile and, in the case of business rates, the relationship between property size and productivity diminishes. Business rate retention does operate a degree of shared income (between state and local authority) and can be considered radical in terms of local government finance in England. However, the system has been left largely untouched since 2013. That change also exposed the challenge of essentially trying to solve fiscal decentralisation through only one tax instrument, rather than a basket of tools and a comprehensive system approach.

- In Germany, expenditure deficiencies and surpluses in revenue are redistributed among municipalities through financial equalisation methodologies which are based on a local authority's financial requirement. This is underwritten in the constitution with principles of adequate finance and the complementary principles of 'connexity' and 'equivalence'. This can be seen in sharp contrast to the shrinking of the revenue support grant and the lack of statutory obligation for equalisation in England.
- Particularly prominent is the coordinating role of the Länder at the state/regional level, which acts as a symbiotic interface between Bund and municipal government in the overall local government finance system. The equivalent tier of government does not exist in England. This so-called missing middle tier of government leaves an ambiguous uncertainty between local state and central state, filled in some areas by mayoral combined authorities.
- Partly in response to high levels of debt in the German local government finance system, a 'debt brake' for sustainable finance was enforced in 2011 alongside transparent auditing procedures for borrowing. The debt brake is a fiscal rule designed to restrict structural imbalances in federal government finances and limit the issuance of government debt. The federal budget is balanced over an economic cycle through a generation of surplus funds during a boom to offset the deficits of the subsequent recession. In the proceeding years, this has begun to wean local authorities away from adverse loan exposure in Germany—particularly for liquidity purposes. In England there has been considerable controversy around borrowing and non-standard investment practices. If adopted in England, a similar process would go some way to providing scrutiny, guidance, and limits for local government investment and borrowing strategies.

References

Beznoska, M., & Kauder, B. (2019). *Debt and investments in municipalities in Germany*. German Economic Institute.

Boettcher, F., Freier, R., Geissler, R., & Niemann, F.-S. (2017). Konsolidierungsprogramme für finanzschwache Kommunen. *Wirtschaftsdienst, 8*, 592–599. https://doi.org/10.1007/s10273-018-2336-1

Bullerjahn, M., & Thöne, J. (2020). *Municipal finance and municipal financial equalisation in Germany*. Deutsche Gesellschaft für Internationale Zusammenarbeit (GIZ) GmbH.

De Widt, D. (2017). The sustainability of local government finances in England, Germany, and The Netherlands: The impact of intergovernmental regulatory regimes. In M. P. R. Bolivar (Ed.), *Financial sustainability in public administration* (pp. 193–225). Palgrave Macmillan.

Färber, G., & Salm, M. (2015). (De-)centralised social transfers and services in Germany: Between central regulation and efficient local allocation. In J. Kim & N. J. Mau (Eds.), *Decentralisation of education, health and social protection: Issues and challenges*. Published by the Korea Institute of Public Finance and the Danish Ministry for Economic Affairs and the Interior.

Geissler, R., Hammerschmid, G. & Raffer, C. Eds (2021) Local public finance: An international comparative regulatory perspective. Springer.

Heinelt, H., & Stolzenberg, P. (2014). 'The Rhinish Greeks'. Bailout funds for local government in German federal states. *Urban Research & Practice, 7*, 228–240. https://doi.org/10.1080/17535069.2014.910934

Insol International. (2022). *When liquidation is not an option: A global study on the treatment of public entities in distress*. Insol International.

OECD. (2022). *World observatory on subnational government finance and investment—Germany*. Retrieved 23, June 2023, from https://www.sng-wofi.org/country-profiles/

Rietzler, K., & Truger, A. (2019). Is the "debt brake" behind Germany's successful fiscal consolidation? A comparative analysis of the "structural" consolidation of the government sub-sector budgets from 1991 to 2017. *Dans Revue de l'OFCE, 2*, 11–30.

Roesel, F. (2017). The political economy of fiscal supervision and budget deficits—Evidence from Germany. *Fiscal Studies, 4*, 641–666. https://www.jstor.org/stable/26605639

Spahn, P. B. (2016). Multi-level finance and the euro crisis. The German experience. In E. Ahmad, M. Bordignon, & G. Brosio (Eds.), *Multi-level finance and the euro crisis* (pp. 83–102). Edward Elgar Publishing.

Zabler, S. (2020). Austerity regimes at the local level: Examining fiscal effects of austerity commissioners using a time-series synthetic control method. *Public Performance & Management Review, 43*(2), 414–432. https://doi.org/10.1080/15309576.2019.1676276

Zabler, S. (2021). New ways of limiting local government debt: An empirical assessment of the German case. In T. Bergström, S. Kuhlmann, J. Franzke, & E. Wayenberg (Eds.), *The future of local self-government. Palgrave studies in sub-National Governance* (pp. 243–256).

Zabler, S. (2022). Uncovering the effect of local government debt brakes in Germany using synthetic controls. *Local Government Studies, 48*(5), 864–886. https://doi.org/10.1080/03003930.2021.1986392

6

Local Government in Italy

Introduction: Political Economy in Italy

In Italy, the path towards local fiscal resilience and autonomy has not been linear, continuous, or without contention. Under the provision of *autonomia differenziata* set out in the amended 2001 Italian Constitution, wealthy north-eastern regions presented a plan for additional devolution and financial autonomy. This brings into question the territorial system of equalisation in Italy because there is an implicit assumption that wealthy locations will retain more of their locally sourced income.

In addition, a long-planned dissolution of the Italian Provinces, as part of an effort towards rationalising frameworks of fiscal federalism, was defeated in a national referendum and declared unconstitutional.

While fiscal equalisation processes exist, Italy's regional structure displays long-standing structural inequality, particularly between the North-East and Southern regions. In the Bolzano-Bozen region, GDP per capita was 2.7 times higher than Calabria in 2020. Consequently, there are significant imbalances in financial resilience and fiscal capacity between regions and their respective municipalities. This is related to the relative buoyancy of the local economy and property markets—the main source

K. Muldoon-Smith et al., *Embedded Autonomy*,
https://doi.org/10.1007/978-981-97-9030-2_6

of municipality revenue. The result is that municipalities with less resource are increasingly reliant on shared tax and intergovernmental transfers to deliver local services and responsibilities.

Italian local government has been reducing its debt burden and improving its financial position following European Union directives, constitutional changes in relation to appropriate debt, balanced budgets, and equilibrium between revenue and expenditure. To some extent, this has slowed the process towards fiscal federalism and local autonomy as the overall government system has concentrated on balance sheet harmonisation, exhibiting again the interrelation of any embedded system of local government financial autonomy and resilience. While there is a general constitutional move towards local financial autonomy and self-reliance, Covid-19 caused a severe reduction in local tax revenue and resulted in significant compensatory central government transfers.

Italian Sub-national Governance Structure

Italy is a parliamentary republic which recognises local and regional autonomy in its constitution. Articles 114 to 133 of the Italian Constitution lay out the basis for sub-national governance set within four layers of government administration:

- Regions
- Provinces
- Metropolitan cities
- Municipalities

According to the OECD Observatory on Sub-National Governance and Investment (2022), the movement towards decentralisation started in the early 1990s with law 142/1990 (the Regulation of Local Autonomies) and then the 1997 Bassanini reform, which laid the foundations for principles of subsidiarity and administrative autonomy—law 59/1997 granted administrative power to the respective regions. Legislative decree 267/2000 enshrined the unified laws on local authorities (Testo Unico). Local autonomy, the application of subsidiarity, and the principle of proportionate financing were then integrated into the reformed constitution of 2001—regions, provinces, and municipalities were given the same status as central government. Article 119 recognised the financial autonomy of regions, provinces, and municipalities and Article 120 stated that central government must provide proportionate finance to deliver devolved functions.

While this reform laid the groundwork for fiscal autonomy, progress has been relatively slow. In response, the Framework Law of 2009 (Law 42/2009) further catalysed progress (recognising Italy as a regionalised country), empowering the Italian government to enact more complete fiscal autonomy (OECD, 2022). In practice, the framework for fiscal autonomy in Italy is based upon an interrelated combination of constitutional principles, legislation, and intergovernmental agreements. Intergovernmental agreements play a major role in moulding fiscal autonomy in Italy—in particular they help define the practical distribution of financial resource, revenue sharing models, and responsibilities. The structure of local government in Italy is shown in Fig. 6.1.

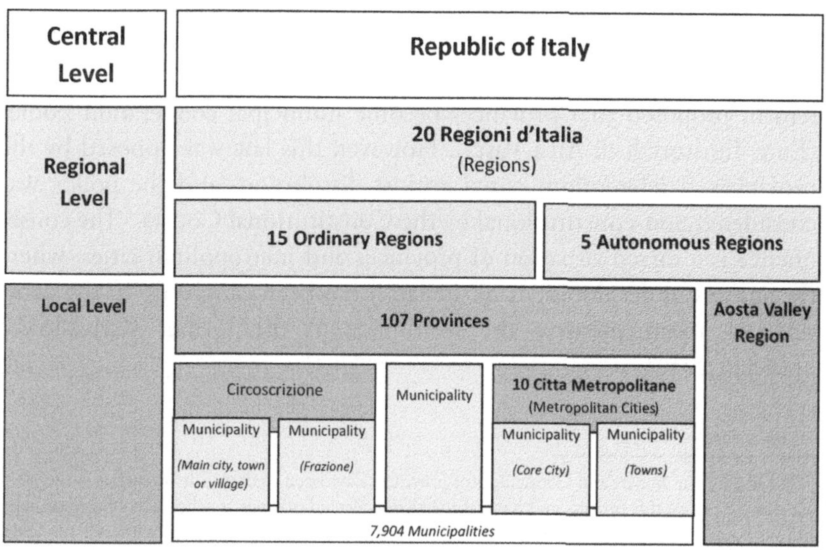

Fig. 6.1 Sub-national governance structure in Italy

Regions have a regional council (Consiglio regionale) and a regional president (Presidente) elected on a five-year term basis. The characteristics of the respective regions is not uniform. Fifteen regions have ordinary status (regioni a statuto ordinario) and five have special status (regioni a statuto speciale)—specifically Sicily, Sardinia, Trentino-Alto Adige, Friuli-Venezia-Giulia, and Valle d'Aosta. These five regions have more legislative power and financial autonomy due to their socio-cultural and geographical characteristics. The Trentino-Alto Adige region is then subdivided further into two autonomous provinces (Bolzano and Trento) which hold the same powers as regions.

In 2009, Rome was given enhanced legal status via Article 24 of Law 42/2009 (Rome capitale) which gave the capital more competencies than a standard city, more fiscal and budgetary power, and additional organisational autonomy. However, the establishment of metropolitan cities (originally enacted in Law 142/1990) has been slow. Law 56/2014 (the Delrio Act) established the legal structure for autonomous governance in the 10 metropolitan cities (citta metropolitana)—Bari, Bologna, Florence, Genoa, Milan, Naples, Reggio Calabria, Rome, Turin, and Venice and four additional cities in the special regions (Catania, Messina, Palermo, and Cagliari). In contrast, provinces have faced an uncertain future in recent decades. Law 56/2014 of the territorial reform laid the groundwork for abolishing the intermediate role of the 107 provinces. The reform proposed that provinces become municipal cooperation bodies (Ente Territoriali di Area Vasta). However, this law was opposed by the provinces, a referendum voted against dissolution, and the policy was considered non-constitutional by the Constitutional Courts.[1] The consequence is a mixed situation of provinces and metropolitan cities, where the successful development of the latter has been caught up in the complicated argument over the legitimacy of the former (Crivello & Staricco, 2017).

[1] Historically, the Mayor and Councillors of provinces have been elected. The intention in the 2014 act was to remove this process and hand it to existing elected officials at other tiers of government. However, elections are still in place today due to the referendum ruling. Nevertheless, the mandate, and the financing of provinces, remains uncertain due to the open and unresolved debate into the nature of provinces.

In early 2023, the Italian government presented a draft law to facilitate the autonomia differenziata—a plan for additional devolution presented by the wealthy northern regions of Emilia-Romagna, Lombardia, and Veneto (Branz, 2023). Under powers in the 2001 amended constitution (under Article 116), in 2018 these northern regions requested extra responsibilities and financial autonomy. This differentiated autonomy has the potential to compromise the system of equalisation, equity, and balanced budgets in Italian local government finance, where the wealthier northern regions traditionally subsidise less buoyant regions in the south (Suwalski & Branz, 2019). This is because northern regions and municipalities exhibit a high share of locally sourced revenues, and southern territories are still reliant on transfers (Ambrosanio et al., 2016). Six further regions have also signed pre-agreements for autonomia differenziata (Piedmont, Liguria, Tuscany, Umbria, Marche, and Campania).

Municipalities are governed by municipal councils (Consiglio) and mayors (Sindaco) elected for five-year terms. Law 142/1990 imposed a minimum size for a new municipality, and this has led to stability in the overall number—as the existing number of municipalities makes it difficult to justify the creation of new municipal entities. However, the population of municipalities vary widely. According to OECD (2022), the average municipal size is 7500 inhabitants, while the median size is 2410 inhabitants. The territorial reform act actively encourages mergers of smaller entities through central and regional incentives. Through financial incentives, Law 142/1990 and Law 56/2014 actively promote intermunicipal cooperation through the development of municipal unions (Unione dei comuni) and mountain communities. Municipal cooperation is compulsory for those locations with less than 5000 inhabitants (there were 562 unions in 2021).

Responsibilities (Shared and Exclusive)

In Italy, responsibilities can be considered across central, regional, and local government. The constitution serves as the basis for the legal system and largely outlines the powers and responsibilities for the respective levels of government. Central government is responsible for foreign policy, defence and social protection, electoral legislation, and overseeing the legal basis for regional and local government. Regions are responsible for healthcare, transport, infrastructure, social services, schools, housing, economic development, and environmental protection.

Regions may also devolve competencies to municipalities through regional legislation. However, municipalities are not governed by regional legislation apart from in the five special status regions. Broadly speaking, municipalities and municipal associations have responsibility for public services, town planning, environment, the local road network, culture and parks, and social welfare. The specific division of responsibilities is presented below.

At the state level, Article 117 of the Italian constitution states that it has exclusive legislative powers in the following matters:

- Foreign policy and international relations of the State; relations between the State and the European Union; right of asylum and legal status of non-EU citizens.
- Immigration.
- Relations between the Republic and religious denominations.
- Defence and armed forces; state security; armaments, ammunition, and explosives.
- The currency, savings protection, and financial markets; competition protection; foreign exchange system; state taxation and accounting systems and equalisation of financial resources.
- State bodies and relevant electoral laws; state referenda; elections to the European Parliament.
- Legal and administrative organisation of the State and national public agencies.
- Public order and security, except for local administrative police.
- Citizenship, civil status, and register offices.
- Jurisdiction and procedural law; civil and criminal law; administrative judicial system.
- Determination of the basic level of benefits relating to civil and social entitlements to be guaranteed throughout the national territory.
- General provisions on education.
- Social security.

- Electoral legislation, governing bodies, and fundamental functions of the municipalities, provinces, and metropolitan cities.
- Customs, protection of national borders, and international prophylaxis.
- Weights and measures; standard time; statistical and computerised coordination of data of state, regional, and local administrations; works of the intellect.
- Protection of the environment, the ecosystem, and cultural heritage.

At the regional level (Regioni), article 117 of the Italian constitution states, "the Regions have legislative powers in all subject matters that are not expressly covered by State legislation". Article 117 of the Italian constitution also outlines areas of concurrent legislation:

- International and EU relations of the Regions.
- Foreign trade.
- Job protection and safety.
- Education, subject to the autonomy of educational institutions and with the exception of vocational education and training.
- Professional learning.
- Scientific and technological research and innovation support for productive sectors.
- Health protection.
- Nutrition.
- Sports.
- Disaster relief.
- Land-use planning.
- Civil ports and airports.
- Large transport and navigation networks.
- Communications.
- National production, transport, and distribution of energy.
- Complementary and supplementary social security.
- Harmonisation of public accounts and co-ordination of public finance and taxation system.
- Enhancement of cultural and environmental properties, including the promotion and organisation of cultural activities.
- Savings banks, rural banks, regional credit institutions.
- Regional land and agricultural credit institutions.

The role of provinces (Provincie) has been significantly reduced over the last decade, when there has been an attempt to shift historic responsibilities (outlined in Legislative Decree 18 August 2000, n.267) to regions or municipalities under Law 56/2014. Regions can legislate regarding how they perform these assigned functions, including attributing competences to the province. The role of provinces is to serve as general-purpose bodies to coordinate the development of their communities.

Provinces have competency in the following areas as outlined in Law 56/2014 Article 1.85:

- Coordination and protection of the environment.
- Planning for transportation services, including private transportation, and managing and regulating the construction and traffic on provincial roads.
- Planning the school system in compliance with regional planning.
- Collecting and processing data and providing technical and administrative assistance to local authorities.
- School building management.
- Monitoring and preventing discrimination in the workplace and promoting equal opportunities within the province.

Law 56/2014 Article 1.86–88 also outlines the following fundamental functions:

- Care of the strategic development of the territory and management of services in associated form based on the specificities of the same territory.
- Care of relations with other forms of government, including stipulating agreements and conventions.
- Preparation of the tender documents of the station contractor, monitoring of service contracts, and organisation of competitions and selection procedures.

Law 56/2014 outlines the general institutional purposes and the fundamental functions of metropolitan cities. The general institutional purposes are:

- Care for the strategic development of the metropolitan territory.
- Promotion and integrated management of services, infrastructures, and communication networks of interest to the metropolitan city.
- Care for institutional relations relating to its level, including those with European cities and metropolitan areas.

As originally conceived, metropolitan cities were responsible for the following fundamental actions:

- Adopting and updating a three-year strategic plan for the metropolitan area, which serves as a guideline for the municipalities within the metropolitan area and for the exercise of functions delegated or assigned by the regions.
- Engaging in general spatial planning, including communication structures, service networks, and infrastructures within the competence of the metropolitan community.
- Structuring coordinated management systems for public services and organising public services of general interest within the metropolitan area.
- Managing mobility and viability and ensuring compatibility and coherence of municipal urban planning within the metropolitan area.
- Promoting and coordinating economic and social development within the metropolitan area, including support for innovative economic and research activities.
- Promoting and coordinating computerisation and digitisation systems within the metropolitan area.

At the municipal (Comuni) scale, Law 42/2009 Article 21 identifies the following fundamental functions:

- Local police.
- Public education for children between 0 and 3 years old.

- Traffic and transport.
- Environment.
- Social services.

Article 13 of Legislative Decree 267/2000 states that municipalities are responsible for all administrative functions that concern their population and territory, "especially in the organic sectors of services to the person and the community, the organisation and use of the territory and economic development except for what is not expressly attributed to other subjects by state or regional law, according to their respective competences". These include:

- Social welfare, in particular personal social services and community assistance.
- Education, including school-related services such as canteens, school buses, assistance for the disabled, preschool childcare, and nursery schools.
- Culture and recreation, including museums, exhibition halls, cultural activities, and theatre.
- Planning, including town planning, housing, and land registry.
- Transport, in particular, running of local transport and maintenance of local roads.
- Economic development, including drafting of plans for trade, planning, programming, and regulation of commercial activities, as well as establishment and management of industrial and trade zones.
- Environment, including waste management.
- Local police.

In Italy, the constitution requires the state to define essential levels of service (LEP) for civil and social rights throughout the country, but there has been a lack of guidance in this sphere. The Constitutional Court has criticised the state's delay in defining these levels; standard requirements have been based on historical service coverage. The National Recovery and Resilience Plan addresses some key areas, such as early childhood education and care services, with dedicated funding until 2026.

The Regulatory Regime

The constitution forms the basis for a system of 'fiscal federalism' (federalismo fiscale). Regions, municipalities, and to some extent provinces and metropolitan cities have powers over local finances. However, the state keeps control of the fundamental principles, laws, and the parameters within which local fiscal autonomy plays out. The legislative framework for the system is grounded in Law 42/2009. The Consolidated Law on Local Authorities (Testo Unico degli Enti Locali—TUEL) is the primary legislation that governs the organisation and operation of municipalities in Italy. It sets out the underlying principles, rules, and procedures for local government finance. The Budget Law (Legge di Bilancio) is a law passed each year by Italian central government that conditions the overall fiscal framework each year. This sets the parameters for local government revenue (e.g., the parameters within which municipalities can alter local tax), expenditure, borrowing, and financial planning and reporting. Both laws set out the revenue sources available to municipalities (including local property tax, a potential portion of personal income tax, fees and charges, and transfers from central government). They also set out the timescales and flexibilities for the preparation and adoption of budgets each year, alongside multi-year financial plans.

This legislative framework also sets out the national accounting standards and regulations, to ensure consistent and comparable financial statements and meaningful scrutiny of municipal finances. In terms of financial control and oversight, the central Ministry of Economy and Finance (MEF) scrutinises local government finance. In practice it is the MEF that sets the accounting standards for municipalities and monitors related financial performance.

In addition, and independently, the Court of Audit (Corte dei Conti) is an independent entity that audits municipal finances, scrutinising financial statements for legality, regularity, and efficiency and sanctioning public officials who have overseen financial irregularities. It is trusted by the constitution in "matters of public accounting" (Article 103, para 2) and supervises all things related to the finance of local governments. Each region also has an audit institution (Corte dei Conte Regionali) that operates under the supervision of the Court of Audit, auditing municipalities in the respective regions. The Court of Audit has a wider remit than the National Audit Office in England. It is actively included in the constitution, taking part in local government fiscal policy development, and involved in the planning of any corrective action: it plays both a consultive and jurisdictional function as a constitutional body. Each year, municipalities must detail their revenue, expenditure, and financial activities for approval from MEF and the Court of Audit. In parallel, municipalities operate internal audit procedures (via Internal Audit Units or Controllers) to scrutinise financial operations—they manage and advise on risk and provide advice on improvements. In practice, this is the municipal strategy for maintaining compliance with the state-based regulatory regime, and internal auditors work in collaboration with the MEF and the Court of Audit.

In addition, the Italian state has a territorial presence based on Prefectures (Prefecture) at the provincial scale,[2] headed by a Prefect (Prefetto). Prefectures are responsible for coordinating and delivering state policy at the local level. The Prefecture works in partnership with municipalities to ensure the proper functioning of local government—for example, ensuring compliance with law and regulation as it relates to financial management. It also plays an important role in liaising and resolving disputes between different levels of government. In this, it can be seen as a key mediating interface for ensuring consistency of approach in relation to state policy at the local scale. The Prefectures also help review and approve the local budget and financial operations. They can intervene if financial regulations have been broken and take control of the municipality.

Under Article 120 of the constitution, central government can intervene in municipal affairs in three circumstances:

- Failure to comply with international rules and treaties or EU legislation.
- A case of grave danger to public safety and security.

[2] In practice province and prefectures are separate entities. Provinces are an autonomous form of sub-national government while prefectures ensure compliance with national policy at the respective territorial scale.

- Whenever action is necessary to preserve legal or economic unity and, in particular, to guarantee the basic level of benefits relating to civil and social entitlements, regardless of the geographical borders of local authorities.

For example, if a municipality faces financial difficulty, central government can impose corrective measures (e.g., debt restructuring or increased local tax levels) to restore financial stability. In addition, under Article 138 of the Testo Unico, the Minister of the Interior has the right to annul the acts of the local authorities. In some circumstances, the state has the power to dissolve local entities entirely and remove local administrators as a sanction. For example, this may be done because a local budget has not been approved in the way prescribed by law. There is also a power to dissolve municipal and provincial councils that are thought to have been undermined by corruption.

Inevitably, in a complicated system of sub-national autonomy and interstate relations, there is demand for a process of negotiation, mediation, and cooperation between the respective tiers of government. The Permanent Conference for Relations between the State and Regions, and the Autonomous Provinces of Trento and Bolzano, commonly known as the State Regions Conference, carries out this role between region and state. The Conference is comprised of representatives from central government, the 19 regional governments, and the autonomous provinces of Trento and Bolzano. The State-Regions Conference provides a forum for central and regional government to discuss, agree, and coordinate revenue-sharing, intergovernmental transfers, and the allocation of specific funds for territorial rebalancing—under the principles of subsidiarity and solidarity. In addition, the Conference plays a role in maintaining central policy consistency across the respective regions (while recognising their territorial difference) and seeks to find consensus in relation to legislative matters. The typical Conference operating procedure is to issue consensus-based agreements, resolutions, and recommendations for regional and central government.

The Local Autonomies Conference (Conferenza della Autonomie) carries out the same role between municipalities and Italian national government. The forum deals with issues related to autonomy, legislation, and financial capacity. The Autonomies Conference is comprised of representatives from the municipalities, provinces, and metropolitan cities. The central role is to safeguard local government interests and autonomy—allowing local governments to raise issues, negotiate with central government, and find consensus around finance and administration. There is also a third conference—the Conferenza Unificata—that joins the regional and local conferences (this conference is established, and the role defined, by Legislative Decree no.28 in 1997). The Constitutional Court (Ruling 31/2006) has recognised that the system of conferences is a key means of implementing the principles of fair co-operation (Congress of Local and Regional Authorities, 2017)—the Prime Minister is the formal chair for the conference, although day to day operation is commonly overseen by the Minister for Regional Affairs and Autonomie. The National Association of Italian Municipalities (ANCI) and the Union of Italian Provinces (UPI) also act, separately, as collective representatives for local levels of government. Alongside the conferences they maintain continuous dialogue with central government in relation to issues impacting local areas while also actively participating in, but not leading, the Local Autonomies Conference.

When consensus cannot be achieved, there is the provision of the respective Constitutional Courts. At the national level, there is the Corte Costituzionale. This Constitutional Court is responsible for ruling on the constitutionality of laws and regulations passed by central government (e.g., the attempt to dissolve provinces). At the local level, each region has a constitutional court, known as the Regional Administrative Tribunal (Tribunali Amministrativi Regionali) which deal with disputes in the regions. These courts are independent judicial bodies and operate under the Council of State (Consiglio di Stato). The Regional Courts have the power to annul or alter local administrative acts that are considered to be non-compliant with national laws and constitutional principles.

Capital Finance

Sub-national government in Italy accounted for 56% of public investment in 2022 (OECDb). The majority of this investment is made by the regions. Following Covid-19 and the Italian Internal Stability Pact, sub-national government investment declined significantly. To manage this deficit in spend, municipalities have received €500 million annually for 2020–2024—to fund small capital works in relation to energy efficiency and sustainable territorial development (OECD, 2022). The state is also making significant funding contributions for regeneration projects, the construction of public buildings, and social infrastructure demands (up to 2034). Following the 2020 Stability Programme, the Italian state also created a territorial investment fund worth €400m per year from 2025 to 2034.

Article 119 of the constitution outlines the 'golden rule' that local authorities can only borrow funds to finance investment expenses. Expanding on this, Article 204 of the TUEL states that local authorities can only take out new loans and other sources of financing if the annual amount of related interest, in addition to the charges already in place (loans previously contracted, bonds previously issued, credit openings stipulated and guarantees given, net total of state and regional interest subsidies), does not exceed a pre-determined level of current revenue.[3]

Local authorities must also comply with the European rules of expenditure control and public debt sustainability. Consequently, Constitutional Law 1/2012 introduced the principle of a balanced budget into the constitution. This requires municipalities to achieve equilibrium between revenue and expenditure in a given period. This reaffirmed the idea that debt can only be used to finance investment expenditure. The law also added that debt can only be proceeded with "the contextual definition of depreciation plans" and on condition that the balanced budget is respected. There is also the possibility of a ban on using debt for investments if the authority fails to attain a balanced budget. This is because of

[3] Decreed by the state, the precise ratio/level has fluctuated yearly between 6% and 10% in recent years as the competing aims of budget harmonisation and local investment need have fluctuated. The Parliamentary Budget Office (Uicio parlamentare di bilancio—UPB), that has autonomy under the 2012 Constitutional Law, has the mandate to scrutinise the balanced budget rule.

specific rules around debt servicing and its relationship with maintaining a balanced budget each year. In reality, the constitutional amendment in 2012 modified the central fiscal federalism principle in articles 117 and 119 to ensure a progressive equilibrium between revenue and expenditure (Gagliano, 2013). In doing so the legislative control over the harmonisation of the public accounts becomes exclusively a state responsibility, presenting in some respects a tension between local autonomy and state oversight. In recent years, there has been some criticism of the limiting impact of the budgeting and scrutiny process. Arguments suggest that the nature and duration of the budgeting process can make it difficult to exploit lending opportunities and to satisfy lender requirements (Ministry of the Interior, 2022a).

In 2022, municipal debt amounted to €32.4 billion, while regions accounted for €39.1 billion and provinces and metropolitan cities €5.6 billion (Banca D'Italia, 2023). Municipalities may issue bonds (known as *obbligazioni degli enti locali*) according to prudential rules—interest below 20% of operating revenue net of healthcare funds for regions; and interest below 10% of operating revenue for local governments (OECD, 2022). Most subnational debt is in the form of bank loans with domestic financial institutions—most notably with the Italian public bank Cassa Depositi e Prestiti. Due to favourable interest rates, this type of loan has increased, while the use of bonds has declined from 30% in 2006 to 6.5% in 2020. If a municipality is going to issue a bond, it must first obtain permission from the MEF after demonstrating financial stability, repayment capacity, and the reason for the issuance. Despite this reduction in use, like Germany, Spain, and France, Italian municipalities remain a major issuer of bonds (OECD, 2022). In addition, while municipalities have benefited from low interest rates for some time, national interest rates have increased considerably in recent years to combat inflation (reaching 3.5% in June 2023, the highest rate since 2001): this represents a major risk in terms of the servicing of respective debt agreements.

Sources of Income

In contrast to England, and like Germany, Italy also has a more structured sub-national governance system. As such the sources of available income and discretion in use must be understood in the context of the sub-national situation and municipal variations (OECD, 2022). In Italy, regions finance their expenditure through their own taxes, their shares of national VAT proceeds, property asset revenue, economic activities, and from equalisation transfers for territories with lower fiscal capacity and debt-based revenue (Brosio, 2018). The main form of tax at the regional scale is the *Imposta Regionale sulle Attivita Produttive* (IRAP), a form of corporate income tax. IRAP is a regional tax levied on net business activity—it is calculated on the basis of the value added by businesses, professionals, and the self-employed (akin to Germany's *Gewerbesteuer*). In addition, regions have the power to levy an additional rate on the Personal Income Tax (the *imposta sui redditi delle persone fisiche*—IRPEF). Both taxes are established and regulated by the state. However, in practice, the tax rates vary from region to region as there is discretion to vary limits within parameters set out by central government.[4]

Since 2001, regions have also received a share of VAT (or *Quota Parte Regionale dell'*IVA) collected within their territorial boundaries for the purpose of financing the national equalisation fund. The President of the Council of Ministers determines the share of VAT which is given to regions. This increased from 38.6% in 2001 to 70.1% in 2020. The VAT powered equalisation fund is used to cover healthcare costs that cannot be covered by local taxation. Regions that are in financial surplus only get to keep a portion of the VAT revenue collected in their own territory, while regions in financial deficit receive the full amount of VAT revenue collected in their territory, plus extra equalisation funds that are not tied to a specific territory.

In terms of local tax, the main municipal tax in Italy is the *Imposta Municipale Propria* or IMU. The IMU can be thought of as primarily a

[4] The IRAP base rate is typically 3.9%—regional authorities can lower rate to 2.98% or increase it to 4.82%. The additional IRPEF rate may be varied between 1.23 and 3.33% between regions.

property tax on residential and commercial property but it also includes taxation for waste (TARI). Historically, there was also the TASI Tax, which accounted for the services that property owners benefited from (such as street lighting)—this has now been merged into the IMU. The IMU operates similarly to the rating system in the UK: it is calculated on the basis of the cadastral value of a given property (the value assigned by the Italian Land Registry) based on the hypothetical income a property would achieve if occupied by a tenant. Different property categories (residential, commercial, agricultural) are given their own tax rate baseline by the Italian state and then municipalities have the power to vary these rates within parameters set by the state. The actual tax is calculated by multiplying the cadastral value by the relative municipal tax rate minus any deductions or exemptions. The tax is levied either on tenants or owner occupiers. Significantly, principal residences are not taxed—second homes and business premises provide the tax yield. In addition, municipalities also have the power to levy an additional surcharge (*Addizionale Comunale*—IRPEF) on the personal income tax rate, alongside the regional surcharge and the national rate. The municipal rate may vary between 0.1% and 0.9%.[5]

Additional taxes can include tourist tax (Tassa di Soggiorno)—levied upon visitors staying in holiday accommodation—and also vehicle tax (including levies on ownership and movement within the territory). Local government in Italy also has the power to instigate charges and fees for waste management, parking, and permits and licenses. These are supplemented by concessions and contracts for public transportation and infrastructure projects as well as revenue from property and land.

Local government in Italy also benefits from central government transfers, including the General Fund (Fondo di Finanziamento Ordinario) and the Equalisation Fund (Fondo di Solidarieta Comunale). The ultimate intention is to fully transition to local sources of revenue and

[5] A recent fiscal reform in 2022 will likely reduce the PIT, revising the rates of the regional and municipal surcharge on PIT and add exemptions to the IRAP for some categories of employment (particularly for self-employed persons). This will disadvantage those regions that have set higher tax rates. In part, the Italian state plans to compensate regions with €8bn in transfers for their healthcare services, since the IRAP represents the main source of financing for the health sector, and it plans a supplementary €76m transfer to compensate regions that applied a higher IRAP rate.

equalisation under fiscal federalism. The General Fund is primarily financed through the national allocation of shared taxes (including Personal and Corporate Income Tax and VAT). It is then distributed on the basis of population size, economic performance, and fiscal capacity—based on the principle of fair and equitable resources across local government in Italy. Practically it is allocated in partnership with the municipal budget planning process and forms a significant part of municipal revenue.

Degree of Own Budgeting and Eccounting

In recent years, regions accounted for 68% of sub-national government expenditure, with municipalities accounting for 30% and provinces and metropolitan cities accounting for the remaining 2%. Health accounted for 49% of overall expenditure. Italy has a rapidly ageing population, and the old age dependency ratio is expected to climb from 39% in 2020 to 67% in 2050 (Lennkh-Yunus, 2023). In the past, this restricted regional autonomy as regions had to finance health spending first through the provision of a 'health pact' with central government. As part of this pact regions had to first ensure a balanced budget in relation to health by funding any deficit through their own reserves and/or via increased local tax. The next largest spending areas were general public affairs, economy and transport, social care, and education. Social care (5%) and education (6%) comprised relatively low contributions to spending as they remain central government responsibilities.

In terms of spending power and revenue, municipalities accounted for 30% of overall sub-national revenue (provinces and metropolitan cities only 2%). In recent years, intergovernmental transfers have accounted for the majority of municipal revenue (OECD, 2022)—61% during Covid-19 due to compensatory measures for Covid-19, up from 47% in 2016. The main source of municipal tax revenue during this period is the IMU property tax, while charges and income accounted for 11%. Table 6.1 describes the breakdown of revenue sources at the municipal level in Italy.

Source: Information based on adjusted numbers from OECD (2022) World Observatory of Sub-National Government Finance and Investment

Table 6.1 Breakdown of local revenue sources in Italy

Revenue Type	% of Income
Transfer Grants (from Central Government)	
Government Transfers: General Fund and Solidarity Fund	61%
(Largely discretionary but elements are earmarked for specific use)	
Taxes (Shared and Local)	
Local Surcharge on Income Tax *(Discretionary in use and rate)*	12% (42% of total local tax)
IMU Property Tax *(Discretionary in use and rate)*	16% (58% of total local tax)
Minor taxes (Dog Tax, Entertainment Tax, Liquor Tax, and Secondary Residence Tax, etc). *(Discretionary in use and rate)*	<1%
Charges and Income	
Charges for water, wastewater, refuse collection and landfill, street cleaning, and various concessions *(Discretionary in use and rate)*	11%
Income from assets	<1%
Other income	<1%
Total Revenue	100%

NB: It is important to note that regions play a significant role in the fiscal autonomy of sub-national government. In terms of fiscal autonomy, regions also benefit from IRAP (the afore-mentioned tax on business activity) a share of VAT and their own levy on personal income tax. The fiscal autonomy of provinces and metropolitan cities, in terms of spending power, is very small

In addition, in recent years the relative share of government transfer has increased due to the impact of Covid-19. This is projected to decrease to closer to 50%—the pre-Covid-19 level

and Italian Ministry of Economic Affairs. The actual spread of revenue in each municipality is variegated due to equalisation and local discretion around taxation

Table 6.1 shows clearly that Italy has a varied basket of taxes at the local level and discretion over rates of taxation and the spending of transferred revenue. Compared with England, Italy has more discretion and flexibility. However, compared with a similarly decentralised governance system, like Germany, it has a less varied basket of revenue sources. For instance, German municipalities receive a share of VAT and levy a tax on business productivity, whereas the latter is collected by the regional tier in Italy. While transferred revenue accounts for a large share of revenue, particularly following Covid-19, Italian municipalities have considerable discretion over its spending. While the overall contribution of property tax appears relatively low (16% of income in the aftermath of Covid-19), it must be noted that the IMU also funds the Municipal Solidarity Fund, the principal means of horizontal territorial equalisation in Italy.

Spending power and fiscal resilience must be understood in tandem with the legislation on the financial distress of municipalities and provinces—codified in Title VIII of Part II, Article 244 of the Consolidated Law on the organisation of local authorities (TUEL). The financial distress and insolvency procedure can be used when a municipality can no longer carry out its basic functions or is unable to discharge liquid and collectable debts. In this case, there is provision to create an extraordinary liquidation body appointed by the President of the Republic after a declaration of financial instability—and a rebalanced budget proposal must be prepared to restore financial stability. In this case, the municipality must work exclusively within the restored budget to avoid future financial instability. The reorganisation of a municipality in this case, including achieving a financial equilibrium, can take up to five years (overseen ultimately by the Ministry of Interior). If the Court of Auditors finds financial mismanagement, irregularities, or imbalances in a local authority's budget, it will set a deadline for corrective measures.

The Regional Audit Sections will identify the necessary measures and verify their adoption. If the entity fails to adopt satisfactory measures, the Court of Auditors will refer the matter to the Prefect and Permanent Conference. They have 30 days to verify the imbalance and assign the Council a maximum of 20 days to resolve bankruptcy. If the Council takes no action, the Prefect will appoint a commissioner to dissolve the council under Article 141 of TUEL. A multi-year financial rebalancing procedure (based on the liabilities to be rebalanced and any unfulfilled commitments) is designed to prevent financial collapse in local authorities by allowing elected bodies to retain management control while being subject to controls to prevent the situation from deteriorating.

The financial stability of Italian municipalities varies significantly. Since the introduction of Law 66/1989, which introduced a procedure of insolvency (Padovani et al., 2018; Ambrosanio et al., 2016), around 8% of Italian municipalities have resorted to the procedure. The vast majority of insolvency procedures and signals of financial distress are in Southern Italy (Ministry of the Interior, 2022b). There are three types of distress: 1) deficit, 2) pre-instability, and 3) failing—the precise rules for governing extreme cases of insolvency are specified in the Testo Unico. Between 2006 and 2016, 102 municipalities have ended up in financial failure, with the majority in Sicily, Campania, and Calabria (Congress on Local and Regional Authorities, 2017).

Method of Territorial Equalisation

Following fiscal federalism, the intention was that local government should fund its obligations from its own tax, and from the proceeds of fiscal equalisation when this is not possible. In Italy there are two forms of equalisation, those related to fundamental obligations and those related to non-fundamental obligations. In terms of fundamental obligations, enabling Law 42/2009 allows for full equalisation of expenditure need. According to Brugnano et al. (2020), standard expenditure needs are used as the benchmark for financing local government—all citizens are guaranteed a minimum level of service. The state defines the essential level of benefits to maintain consistency between territory.[6] The state distinguishes between fundamental functions at the local level (that receive full financing) and remaining local functions (which receive only partial equalisation in fiscal capacity).

The gap, defined by the difference between spending need and fiscal capacity, is filled via the vertical redistribution of state resources. In relation to non-fundamental obligations, the same enabling law allows for partial equalisation of expenditure funded horizontally via the tax

[6] Legislative Decree 216/2011 defined the list of fundamental functions and gave guidance on the monitoring of these functions via the collection of local government data. In reality, benchmarks are ambiguous and rarely evident. In particular, the essential levels of benefit have never been defined and the result that historical spending is still used as a benchmark on a regular basis.

resources from wealthy municipalities—the primary revenue for achieving this is the local property tax (Brosio, 2018). In reality, there is increasingly very little vertical redistribution and almost all equalisation is horizontal. This is largely because the enabling law specifies that central transfers should not exceed historical costs and should not create additional costs for the state.

The Municipal Solidarity Fund (Fondo di Solidarietà Comunale) is the most important equalisation method for municipalities. The fund was created by Law 228/2012 and first implemented in 2013. It is managed by the Ministry of Economy and Finance and the National Association of Italian Municipalities (ANCI). Both institutions define the allocation formula and monitor its implementation. The central principle of the fund is solidarity; poorer municipalities should be cross-subsidised by more affluent municipalities (Corte dei Conti, 2019; Bucci et al., 2023). The total size of the Municipal Solidarity Fund in 2021 was €6.6bn and it is set to be increased yearly up to €7.7bn in 2030 (OpenCivitas, 2022).

Funds are allocated on the principle of equalisation and in part to offset historical figures relating to municipalities' own income and transfers, with the final target being to abandon historical expenditure as a means of revenue distribution. Criteria are centred around the difference between fiscal capacity and expenditure need; the aim is that by 2030, 100% equalisation will have been achieved. As of 2022, the percentage of the fund distributed in line with equalisation criteria is 60%, with the remainder based upon the traditional model of historical spending. In 2019, 93% of municipalities received a positive balance from the fund—those with a negative transfer (those distributing their income to fund less buoyant locations) are primarily located in the north and centre of the country, reflecting those areas' local wealth and self-sufficiency (474 municipalities paid resources into the Municipal Solidarity Fund compared with 6054 beneficiaries).

The theoretical outcome is that transfers from central government are almost entirely designed for equalisation purposes. Ring-fencing is deemed unconstitutional. The exception to this rule is when the government system is operating under exceptional circumstances, for example, during Covid-19 and in its aftermath, when central government increased the total fund using state resources. These funds were ring-fenced for the performance of social functions, particularly relating to strengthening social services, the expansion of some nursery services, and school transport for disabled pupils. There is now some ambiguity in relation to whether these central resources will remain in place. While the intention of fiscal federalism in Italy is to allow for self-sufficiency, there is a practical difference between this intention and the implementation of true autonomy and territorial equality (Raffer & Padovani, 2020). The result is a continual element of state funding to achieve equalisation and minimum service provision. This is particularly acute during financial distress and cyclical economic activity, when the local tax base, held locally and redistributed territorially, varies.

Summary

The following observations can be made about the Italian local government finance system, as it relates to the potential for change in England:

- The Italian local government finance system also displays the components of a complex adaptive system and exhibits attributes of embodied autonomy seen in the previous case of Germany. However, the Italian path towards fiscal autonomy and resilient local government financing is more recent than the German case. The Italian case must be seen in the context of competing themes of fiscal autonomy: the European Union demand for balanced budgets, and consequent austerity and financial restructuring in Italian government; historical economic underperformance and regional inequality; and additional cost pressures due to Covid-19, the current geo-political situation, and inflation. All of these narratives impact on local government financial management and are very similar to the situation currently faced in England.
- In contrast to England, in the main, the problem of unfunded mandates does not exist in Italy. While the availability and buoyancy of local income does vary, it is rare to find any mismatch between trans-

ferred powers and the means to pay for them. This is because the movement towards fiscal federalism has evolved under the principles of subsidiarity, proportionate finance, and territorial solidarity. This can be seen in contrast to England, where some powers have been devolved to different tiers of government, but recent debates over sources of finance have been entirely detached from function, proceeding on parallel lines. This is because sub-national government in England, as a specific entity, does not have any codified role. The proliferation of unfunded mandates in England can be seen as the consequence of the power hierarchy inherent in the British political tradition (Rodríguez-Pose & Gill, 2003; Rodríguez-Pose & Vidal-Bover, 2022).

- Italian municipal revenue is more diverse than that of England, with municipalities receiving a higher share of their revenues through local and shared tax. Municipalities have power to levy tax on property and personal income. They can also vary (upward and downward) these taxes within nationally prescribed parameters and laws. In contrast, the English system is grounded upon grants provided by central government. The reliance on property tax, in both Italy and England, presents a risk as property markets become more volatile and, in the case of business rates in England, as the relationship between property size and productivity diminishes.
- While the Italian constitution presents a firm basis for the allocation of competencies between different tiers of government, the reality is that there is significant overlap between their responsibilities (Raffer & Padovani, 2020). This separation of function can be considered as a set of general guidelines drawn up as Italy moved from the principle of uniformity to the principle of differentiation—where different kinds of local authorities have the ability to carry out tasks differently in contrasting areas of the country (Boggero, 2016).
- In reality, there is a great deal of negotiation, and the need for continual consensus building, in relation to respective responsibility and the related means of payment. This negotiation is facilitated by a rich territorial system of conferences, municipal associations, the Court of Auditors, the local prefecture, and the Constitutional Courts who all actively interpret, protect, and embed the principles of local

autonomy. In contrast, England has at best a disjointed and partial system of territorial mediation and oversight. Its National Audit Office (NAO) has an independent national remit to audit the public accounts, and to assess value for money—reporting this information to Parliament via the Public Accounts Committee. The NAO, while effective, does not have local government as part of its remit. The Audit Commission, the local government equivalent, was abolished in 2015 and its responsibilities divided among several organisations (Ferry, 2019).

- Not all municipalities and regions in Italy are in favour of fiscal autonomy. Less wealthy locations are inevitably more in favour of revenue sharing, while those with more wealth argue in favour of more local retention. In addition, regions argue for the power to allocate resources to municipalities, while municipalities prefer a direct relationship with central government—as the state is considered more financially viable and politically fair (Brosio, 2018). Parallels can be seen in England where central London authorities and the core cities in England regularly call for the capacity to retain more of their own income. This reveals the often-hidden reality that fiscal decentralisation and autonomy is not a panacea for the challenges of local government finance in England: it is a contested and varied instrument.
- Nor is the implementation of fiscal autonomy straightforward. In Italy, De Siano and D'Uva (2017) argue that the process started in the 1970s with the transfer of administrative functions to ordinary statute regions (Law no. 281/1970). The transition to fiscal federalism, instigated by the Fiscal Federalism Framework in 2009, is projected to last until at least 2030—as the system of local government finance transitions from historical finance practices to the new system, which is based on formula grants. At the same time referendum results, in relation to provinces, have questioned the fabric and rationale underpinning the territorial basis for fiscal decentralisation (Congress of Local and Regional Authorities, 2017).

References

Ambrosanio, M. F., Balduzzi, P., & Bordignon, M. (2016). Economic crisis and fiscal federalism in Italy. In E. Ahmad, M. Ambrosanio, & G. Brosio (Eds.), *Multi-level finance and the euro crisis* (pp. 212–246). Edward Elgar.

Banca D'Italia. (2023). *Local government debt: Statistics.*

Boggero, G. (2016). The establishment of metropolitan cities in Italy: An advance or a setback for Italian regionalism? *Perspectives on Federalism, 8*(3), 1–22. https://doi.org/10.1515/pof-2016-0014

Branz, J. (2023). *Italy: Regional devolution plan could exacerbate divides, test predictability of public finances.* Scope Ratings. European Rating Agency.

Brosio, G. (2018). Ambition beyond feasibility? Equalization transfers to regional and local governments in Italy. *Budget and Public Expenditure, 92*, 135154.

Brugnano, C., Ferraina, G., Loi, F., Minzyuk, L., & Nitti, M. (2020) *Fiscal federalism and equalisation design under the growing public finance constraint: A case of Italian municipalities.* MPRA Paper 102001, University Library of Munich.

Bucci, V., Ferrara, G., & Resce, G. (2023). Local government spending efficiency and fiscal decentralization: Evidence from Italian municipalities. *Applied Economics, 56*(5), 599–614. https://doi.org/10.1080/00036846.2023.2169241

Congress on Local and Regional Authorities. (2017, October 18). *Local and regional democracy in Italy.* Monitoring Committee. Council of Europe.

Corte dei Conti. (2019, dicembre 11). *Audizione della Corte dei Conti sui Sistemi Tributari delle Regioni e degli Enti Territoriali nella prospettiva dell'attuazione del Federalismo Fiscale e dell'Autonomia Differenziata, VI COMMISSIONE PERMANENTE FINANZE.*

Crivello, S., & Staricco, L. (2017). Institutionalising metropolitan cities in Italy. Success and limits of a centralistic, simplifying approach. *Urban Research & Practice, 10*(2), 228–238. https://doi.org/10.1080/17535069.2017.1307001

De Siano, R., & D'Uva, M. (2017). Fiscal decentralisation and spillover effects of local government public spending: The case of Italy. *Regional Studies, 51*(10), 1507–1517. https://doi.org/10.1080/00343404.2016.1208814

Ferry, L. (2019). *Audit and inspection of local authorities in England: Five years after the local audit and accountability act 2014*. Communities and Local Government Committee.

Gagliano, A. (2013). The introduction of the 'balanced budget' principle into the Italian constitution: What perspectives for the financial autonomy of regional and local governments? *Perspectives on Federalism, 5*(1), 79–96. https://ssrn.com/abstract=2421383

Lennkh-Yunus, Y. (2023). *Italian Republic rating report*. Scope Ratings for the Sovereign and Public Sector.

Ministry of the Interior. (2022a). *The investments of local authorities: Trend analysis and actions per ilrilancio*. Ministry of the Interior.

Ministry of the Interior. (2022b). *Financial critical issues of local authorities: Causes and points of reflection for a reform of prevention and remediation procedures*. Observatory on the Finance and Accounting of Local Authorities—Rome.

OECD. (2022). *World observatory on subnational government finance and investment—Italy*. Retrieved 23, June 2023, from https://www.sng-wofi.org/country-profiles/

OpenCivitas. (2022). *The allocation of the municipal solidarity fund*. OpenCivitas—Ministry of Local Government Finance.

Padovani, E., Rescigno, L., & Ceccatelli, J. (2018). Municipal bond debt and sustainability in a non-mature financial market: The case of Italy. *Sustainability, 10*, 1–25. https://doi.org/10.3390/su10093249

Raffer, C., & Padovani, E. (2020). Italy report. In R. Geissler, G. Hammerschmid, & C. Raffer (Eds.), *Local public finance in Europe: Country reports*. Bertelsmann Stiftung and Hertie School of Governance.

Rodríguez-Pose, A., & Gill, N. (2003). The global trend towards devolution and its implications. *Environment and Planning C: Government and Policy, 21*(3), 333–351. https://doi.org/10.1068/c0235

Rodríguez-Pose, A., & Vidal-Bover, M. (2022). Unfunded mandates and the economic impact of decentralisation. When finance does not follow function. *Political Studies, 72*(2), 652–676. https://doi.org/10.1177/00323217221136666

Suwalski, J., & Branz, G. (2019). *Italian regions' autonomy plans weigh on the fiscal framework's predictability*. Scope: Scope Ratings.

7

Local Government in Japan

Introduction: Political Economy in Japan

Japan has a long held demographic challenge associated with an ageing population and fewer young people entering the economy, leading to an increasing dependency ratio and increased concern around the sustainability of public finances. In addition, Japan is traditionally prone to a variety of natural disasters. The local government finance system must allocate resources to prepare for and manage the aftermath of such situations.

There are significant disparities in localised revenue in Japan, particularly relating to the collection of local tax. The disparity is seen particularly between urban and rural areas, with the latter suffering from declining population and less buoyant tax bases. In addition, while Japan has access to several sources of local tax revenue (compared with England), the system itself is seen in some quarters as inflexible, with central government defining the parameters of local taxation; and it is also heavily reliant on property tax and local consumption tax. The result is a local government finance resource base that is very dependent on the local economy.

K. Muldoon-Smith et al., *Embedded Autonomy*,
https://doi.org/10.1007/978-981-97-9030-2_7

Large fiscal transfers from central to local government are necessary to ensure uniform service provision (according to national baselines). Local sources of revenue play a limited role in balancing the inter-territorial budget, as the proportion of local finance that they make up is relatively fixed. In some quarters this equalisation procedure is seen as limiting fiscal autonomy and vulnerable to changing government priorities and politics. Even though there is a mature process of equalisation in place, the maintenance of an even and proportionate system of local government finance in Japan is an ongoing challenge. When increases in local sources of revenue are evident, this can lead to a reduction in central transfers. The result is a potential disincentive for local authorities increasing their own local revenue, as central transfers can provide more certainty.

Some local governments in Japan have significant debt burdens associated with historical investment in public infrastructure, social welfare programmes, and the need to fund the demands of fiscal decentralisation (Doshu-sei Kaikaku) since the early 2000s. Coupled with declining revenue sources (particularly in rural areas), the servicing of debt while maintaining essential services is increasingly challenging. The Japanese central government, led by the Ministry of Internal Affairs and Communication (MIC), has introduced debt consolidation initiatives, enhanced fiscal rules set out in the Local Finance Act (Chihou Koukuu Hou) and tighter central control measures.

Japanese Subnational Governance Structure

The local government finance system in Japan is designed to provide essential public services and promote local development while ensuring fiscal sustainability. Again, evoking the core principles in this book of embedded autonomy and system-based resilience, this process balances the constitutional emphasis on autonomy of local government with the requirement of central coordination, oversight, and overall financial resilience. Japan has a three-tier system of government (national, regional, and local) embedded in and supported by a multi-level sub-national governance system (see Fig. 7.1). There are 47 Prefectures in Japan. These are divided into one To (Tokyo), one Do (Hokkaido), two Fu (Osaka and

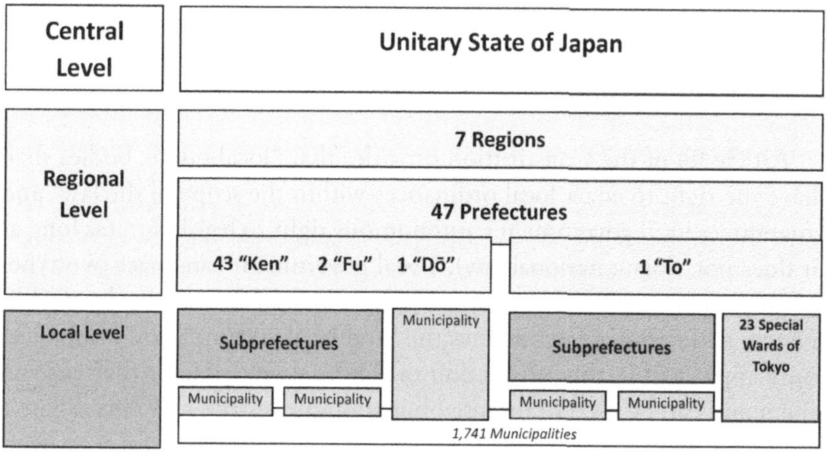

Fig. 7.1 Structure of sub-national governance in Japan

Kyoto), and the other 43 are referred to as Ken. They are the biggest administrative unit in Japan and have their own governor and elected assembly. Cities (Shi) are the second biggest administration unit and are traditionally classified (typically on the basis of population and economy) into designated cities (Tokurei Shi), core cities (Chukan Shi), special cities (Tokubetsu Shi), and ordinary cities (Futsu Shi). Each city has its own mayor and city council. More recently, the classification of special cities and core cities have been merged. The lowest levels of administrative governance are found at the town (Machi) and village (Mura). These levels provide local governance to rural and less populated areas.

Local autonomy in Japan is constitutionally protected and considered indispensable to democracy. Chapter 8 of the Constitution, adopted in 1946, contains four articles outlining the nature and guarantee of local autonomy:

- Article 92: outlines the basic "principle of local autonomy".
- Article 93: established legislative assemblies and the direct election of local officials.
- Article 94: details that local public entities shall have the right to manage their property, affairs, and administration and to enact their own regulations within law.

- Article 95: details the requirement of a referendum to apply a special law that is only applicable to one local public entity—the Local Autonomy Special Law.

Article 94 of the Constitution provides that "local public bodies shall have the right to enact local ordinances within the scope of the law" and guarantees local government's autonomous right to legislation (as long as it does not violate national law). Local government can enact two types of laws: ordinances and regulations. The relationship between local ordinances and national laws defines the local legal system. Local ordinances only apply within the jurisdiction of the local government that enacted them and can be used to impose obligations or restrict residents' rights.

Through the system of local democracy, residents can perform an oversight role of local authorities. These include:

- Direct petition.
- Petition to enact, revise, or abolish local ordinances. Petitions related to local taxes and usage of charges are not allowed.
- Petition to audit government activities. The petition compels the audit committee of the local government to determine whether or not the affairs of the local government in question are being properly carried out. Results must be announced publicly.
- Petition for dissolution of the assembly. Requires the signatures of one-third or more of eligible voters.
- Petition for removal of assembly members.
- Petition for removal of the chief executive, etc.

Other forms of participation:

- Referenda concerning local autonomy special laws: a local autonomy special law must be approved by a majority vote of residents.
- Petition by residents for audit and lawsuit: residents can petition members of the audit committee to conduct audits seeking information on suspected illegal or improper disbursements of official funds, acquisition, management or disposition of properties, and execution of contracts by the staff of the local government. Residents who are

unsatisfied with the audit outcome can bring a lawsuit. A petition of this kind may be signed by one person.

The guarantee to local government of the autonomous right to legislation in Japan allows local authorities to create and enforce their own laws, known as ordinances and regulations. The system allows for greater flexibility in making decisions on what impacts a local community. In England, local government has much less legislative authority, restricted mostly to the enactment of bylaws, and it has no residential petition system.

The Local Autonomy Law, which was adopted in 1947, is the cornerstone for the basic operation of local government in Japan, outlining matters such as types, powers, legislative assemblies, agencies, and financial affairs. It also outlines the vertical intergovernmental relationship between state and local government and also the horizontal relationship between respective local governments. The law came into effect in 1947, concurrently with the constitution.

The Local Autonomy Law specifies two basic types of local authority: prefectures and municipalities. Prefectures are regional government units and municipalities are the basic local government unit. Prefectures and municipalities operate as independent entities that carry out local public administration within their jurisdictions—both entities have democratically elected governing bodies and representatives. The system is centred on the comprehensive authorisation principle; prefectures and municipalities act as comprehensive administrative bodies and perform activities considered necessary for their residents.

Japan has seen a decrease in the number of municipalities since they were first introduced in 1888 (OECD, 2022). Broadly speaking, there have been three periods of merger. The first was the 'Great Meiji Consolidation' in which roughly 70,000 cities, towns, and villages were merged into 15,000 entities. The second period, the 'Great Showa Consolidation', took place from 1953 to 1961 and reduced the number of municipalities by around two-thirds. The most recent reform has been underway since 1999 in the midst of a background of local financial difficulties and Japan's attempt to become more decentralised. Between 1999 and 2020, the number of municipalities decreased from 3229 to 1718. As the number of municipalities decreased, their respective administrative and financial powers increased, as well as their capabilities necessary to deal with issues associated with social and economic development.

The Local Autonomy Law classifies local government into two categories: ordinary local government and special local government. Ordinary local governments, including prefectures and municipalities, are entities that operate independently without hierarchy. However, they have distinct functions: prefectures are large-scale governments covering multiple municipalities, while municipalities are smaller and more connected to residents' daily lives. Although prefectures offer advice and guidance to municipalities, they also perform licensing and permit functions from a regional perspective.

There is also a 'special local government' system. These do not exist everywhere and are entities with unusual geographic areas, organisational structures, or powers. The first entity under this principle is the 23 'special wards', which are all located within Tokyo. These wards carry out narrower duties than cities but serve the same function. In Tokyo, some functions that the city would usually carry out are the responsibility of the Tokyo Metropolitan Government. Examples include firefighting, fresh water supply, and sewage. The second type of specialised entity is called 'local public cooperatives', which are organisations formed by two or more local authorities to address a particular issue with greater efficiency and effectiveness. These are classified into two types: 'partial cooperatives', which manage waste disposal, fire services, etc., and 'wide-area cooperatives', which create plans for matters that span large areas. The last specialised entity is called 'property wards', which manage the property and facilities owned by a municipality. However, these are typically only found in agricultural or mountain villages.

In addition to the cooperatives, there is also a thriving range of local government associations in Japan that work towards cooperative interstate relations, work with national government to shape financial settlements, advocate the interests of local government regionally and nationally, share best practice, and, more broadly, help to address common challenges around local government finance. For example, the Japan Association of City Mayors drives collaboration among major urban areas; the Japan Association of Prefectural Governors represents Japan's

47 prefectures and coordinates cooperation and response to national policy directives; the Japan Association of City Councils enhances cooperation between local government and advocates for the principles of local autonomy; the Council of Local Authorities for International Relations encourages and assists with international exchange and partnership working at the local level; and at the lowest level of government there is the National Association of Chairpersons of Towns and Villages that promotes the interests of towns and villages in Japan and seeks partnership between the smallest scale of government.

Supporting all tiers of government, there is also the Japan Municipal Bond Council that helps advise the issue of municipal bonds in Japan. It plays a key role in driving good practice and transparency in the municipal bond market. Finally, there is also a rich tradition of Municipal Research and Training Institutes (typically funded by prefectures and municipalities) that provide research and training for local government officials and overall capacity building for prefectures and municipalities.

The sub-national system of government in Japan can be described as a 'fusion-type system' (Machidori, 2023) in which central and local administrative entities exist in a mutually dependent and mutually complementary relationship. Decentralisation in Japan is rooted in the Local Autonomy Law (Chihou Jichi Hou) and other relevant laws amended by the Comprehensive Local Autonomy Law enacted in July 1999. Prior to then, the local government system in Japan could be compared to the current situation in England, dominated by a range of delegated agency functions. The reforms implemented included:

- Classification of roles to be carried out by national and sub-national governments: the central government should focus on international duties and matters requiring a unified approach, while local government should handle tasks more closely related to residents' daily lives.
- Abolition of the system of delegated functions and restrictions on involvement by national administrative agencies. The local government's chief executive is no longer seen as a lower administrative agency of the national government. National administrative agencies are also no longer allowed to interfere with local government unless permitted by law or ordinance (the "statutory involvement principle").

- National powers were transferred to prefectures, and powers of prefectures were transferred to municipalities.

The Local Autonomy Act, which defines the relationship between national and local government, provides an objective foundation for any dispute between the respective tiers of government. There is also a Local Autonomy Committee (Chihou Jichi Chousaki) hosted by the Ministry of Internal Affairs. This committee investigates (via referral) disputes between local and central government, providing a forum for their resolution. While this forum has no official powers (it is seen as an advisory body), it makes recommendations for efficient amelioration of problems and has significant standing in interstate relations in Japan. As in Germany, when resolution cannot be found, it is possible for local government (individually or collectively) to take legal action against central government through a system of judicial review.

Responsibilities (Shared and Exclusive)

While countries like Germany and Italy have codified lists of local government responsibilities in their constitution and associated legislation, Japan's constitution (the Nihonkou Kenpo) falls short in this respect. While it defines the structure of governance it does not specifically list respective functions. The Local Autonomy Act goes further, outlining responsibilities and functions, and establishes the overall framework for local governance—acting as a fundamental law that outlines the principles of local government. However, it was not until more recently that local government responsibilities were given more clarity through the Law for the Improvement of Relevant Laws for the Promotion of Decentralization, enacted in July 1999 (also known as the Omnibus Local Autonomy Law). The law makes central government responsible for the following:

- Affairs relating to Japan as a nation in the international community.
- Affairs relating to various activities of the people that should be handled in a uniform, nationwide manner.

- Executing policies and projects that must be performed from a nationwide viewpoint or on a nationwide scale.

The law stipulates that local government is primarily responsible for carrying out administrative tasks within their respective regions autonomously and comprehensively, with as much local autonomy as possible. Previously Japan operated around a system of delegated agency functions, but this was abolished with the 'Omnibus Local Autonomy Law' amendment.

The functions of local government are divided into two types. The first is 'statutory entrusted affairs'; these are functions entrusted to local government through legislation and were originally the responsibility of central government, which retains responsibility for ensuring proper implementation. These include issuing passports, management of national roads, and statistical affairs for central government. All functions which are not 'statutory entrusted' are known as 'local autonomy functions'. These 'autonomous functions' can be further categorised into 'statutory' and 'discretionary' responsibilities.

While subsidiarity is not explicitly mentioned in Japanese local government institutions, the principle can be seen as implicit in the allocation of responsibilities. The 'principle of municipal priority' lies at the heart of the allocation of functions between prefectures and municipalities. The Local Autonomy Law designates that prefectures, as a regional tier of government, oversee wide-scale regional affairs, communication and coordination relating to municipalities, and supplementary affairs for municipalities. Municipalities are then responsible for affairs not covered by prefectures. Fundamentally, functions are allocated first to municipalities, then prefectures, and only then to the central government if the sub-national government cannot perform a task. However, the actual allocation of affairs is not always straightforward, prefectures and municipalities, in many cases, cannot completely separate out functions between the relevant entities. This is why the approach to the allocation of affairs in Japan is referred to as the 'fusion type' in the local autonomy system, as opposed to the 'separation type' (Machidori, 2023).

The responsibilities of prefectures are as follows:

- Wide-area affairs (e.g., prefectural roads, harbours, forest and river conservation, public health centres, vocational training, police).
- Communication and coordination affairs relating to municipalities (e.g., advice, recommendations and guidance concerning rationalisation of municipal organisation and operations).
- Supplementary affairs for municipalities (e.g., high schools, museums, hospitals).

The responsibilities of municipalities are as follows:

- Affairs relating to the fundamentals of residents' lives (e.g., family registers, resident registration, street addresses).
- Affairs relating to ensuring the safety and health of residents (e.g., fire service, garbage disposal, water supply, sewage).
- Affairs relating to the welfare of residents (e.g., public assistance (within the area of cities), nursing insurance, national health insurance).
- Affairs relating to urban development plans (e.g., urban design, municipal roads, parks).
- Affairs relating to the establishment and management of various facilities (e.g., public halls, citizens' halls, day-care facilities, elementary and junior high schools, libraries).

The Regulatory Regime

The local government finance system in Japan is committed to providing stable public services regardless of regional differences (Japanese Ministry of Finance, 2023; Council of Local Authorities for International Relations, 2022). To achieve this, central government formulates the Local Government Finance Plan (LGFP) each year based on a relative needs assessment of local government finance and forecasts of overall revenue and expenditure in parallel with national budget plans. Under this initiative, all local government revenue sources (including local allocation tax grants, bonds, and loans) are accounted for in such a way that sufficient funding is available for uniform public services to be delivered. Historically, the Local Autonomy Act laid out the basis for matters relating to local government finance (Bessho, 2016), establishing the framework for fiscal autonomy and local financial management. Other important acts include the Local Finance Law (Chiho Zaisei Hou), the Local Tax Law (Chiho Zei), and the Local Public Services Law (Chiho Komuin). Concurrently, local government exists within a set of fiscal discipline rules and budgetary control measures.

Local authorities must prepare multi-year fiscal plans and publish annual financial statements and budgets detailing revenue, expenditure, and the overall financial state of play. This is a key facet of maintaining transparency and accountability to the general public. Independent Local Government Audit Boards (Chihou Kyoukyoku Danntai Keisan Kansa Iinkai) review the financial statements and the general system resilience of the local government finance operations, ensuring that the local government finance system is adhering to fiscal laws and regulations—particularly in relation to budget, revenue collection, and expenditure management. The boards are a key mechanism in proactively preventing local government insolvency and managing financial problems. While there is no legal basis for local government insolvency in Japan, it has occasionally happened (see the Yubari case in Hokkaido described later in this section). However, insolvency is very rare with fiscal discipline and financial scrutiny preventing systemic insolvency. When problems are evident, the Local Finance Law sets out the principles for collaborative solutions and responsible management, avoiding formal insolvency measures.

The legal basis for independent local government audit boards is set out in the Local Autonomy Law which details the composition, role, and the boards' overall powers. The local audit boards operate in association with the national Board of Audit of Japan (Chosaki), which scrutinises the national financial position while supporting local audit boards in relation to auditing standards and conventions. The audit boards then share their assessment with the relevant local government entity and publish their findings and recommendations in the public domain. This represents another layer of public accountability in the local government system, ensuring that public funds are managed correctly and that investors have confidence in the soundness of a given local government entity.

In addition, central government, via the Ministry of Public Affairs and Communication and the Local Finance Law, polices tight limits in relation to borrowing and fiscal planning. The Local Finance Law sets out the framework for fiscal discipline, transparency, and accountability. There are strict limits in relation to the quantity of debt, and its servicing, that can be held at any given time and specific rules for the issuance of bonds held under the overall principle of sustainable debt levels and excessive debt accumulation. There is quite a lot of flexibility in relation to the type of bonds available for issuance, including no obligation bonds, revenue bonds, and project-specific bonds. However, before incurring any debt a given local government must get approval from their local assembly (similar to a local authority council in England) while the budget must clearly stipulate the purpose of debt, its quantity, and the repayment strategy. The local assembly ensures that locally elected representatives have a say in the financial planning of local authorities and helps make sure that any issuance of debt is reviewed in light of the overall local government budget, financial health, and relevant policy priorities.[1]

Traditionally, the financial management of local government was conducted under the Law on Special Measures for the Promotion of Local Financial Reconstruction (Chihou Zaisei Saiken Sokushin Tokubetsu Sochi Hou). This law was the central framing legislation between 1955 and 2009 (Hirota & Yunoue, 2022). This former fiscal rule only focused on the ordinary accounts of local government, ignoring debt and investment—therefore only a partial picture of financial resilience was evident. In addition, some local governments could draw on their reserves (kept for the repayment of future debt) to make their accounts appear healthier, while there was capacity to move ordinary account fiscal deficits to extra-governmental accounts.

Under the previous system, the Japanese government operated a 'red card' system for local governments in need of financial reconstruction based on a deficit index (Jisshitsu Akaji Hiritsu). Local governments falling under this definition had to operate under the control of central government (the Ministry of Internal Affairs and Communication) to recover

[1] There is an extra layer of oversight and permission, via the Ministry of Internal Affairs and Communication, for those local authorities in financial distress.

financial health and were not allowed to issue bonds (Hirota & Yunoue, 2022). The former process was criticised for having no graduated process (a yellow card system) that could avoid the need for 'fiscal reconstruction'. The result was a system that could only act once a given local government was in a structural state of distress—lacking curative or preventative distress management mechanisms (Hirota & Yunoue, 2022).

Following the insolvency of the city of Yubari in 2007, in 2008, the Law Relating to the Financial Soundness of Local Governments (Chihou Koukyoudantai no Zaisei no Kenzenka ni Kansuru Houritsu) was enacted, referred to as the new fiscal rule (Hirota & Yunoue, 2022). Similarly to England, the Japanese system of insolvency does not recognise the bankruptcy of local government—however Yubari had debts of 35bn JPY against an annual budget of only 4bn JPY (Seaton, 2010). The new law is based on a revised and expanded set of financial indexes, a Deficit Index (covering ordinary accounts), a Consolidated Deficit Index (which includes the accounts of additional public enterprises), the Redemption Index (which includes local government debt), and the Future Burden Index (which includes all public entities in each municipality). Taken together, these financial reporting tools attempt to create an overall picture of local government financial resilience while the Future Burden Index serves to understand the potential for financial distress in the future. This wider scrutiny has created the scope for a 'yellow card' system, requiring local governments to put plans in place for financial recovery, while a 'red card' requires local governments to be under central control while financial soundness is recovered.

Confronted by these situations, a local public finance reform called the "Trinity Reform" was introduced in 2006. The reform aimed to promote further decentralisation, increase the freedom of local government to implement revenue and expenditure strategies, and to foster more local government fiscal independence from central government. The underlying rationale in the promotion of the "Trinity Reform" was the belief that one of the central root causes of severe local government financial distress lay in the weak capacity of local government to generate and/or have discretion over its own tax revenue and income. In order to respond to this criticism, the reform revised the financial transfer scheme to expand the number of local revenues—including local taxes and assigned taxes traditionally held by central government. The whole reform process, initiated in 2003, transferred and streamlined the operation of the tax model for the Local Allocation Tax and the National Treasury Disbursement to local government. It is estimated that the Japanese Government transferred three trillion JPY (some £13 billion) to local government in 2006.

Capital Finance

The three major sources of bonds/borrowing in Japan are the private sector, government bonds, and those provided by the Japanese Finance Organisation for Municipalities (JFM). The JFM is a joint fundraising organisation for local government which raises funds in the capital market, and then provides long-term loans at low interest rates to local government. Compared with England, the range of borrowing-based activities is wider. For example, bonds can be issued to cover expenses for publicly owned corporations, disbursements, and loans, refinancing of local bonds, disaster emergency projects, and maintenance of public facilities.

While the Japanese local government finance system does not have the same debt restrictions as those countries operating under the European Union fiscal rules, the Japanese government does, in effect, guarantee any local government borrowing via a system of intergovernmental budget setting and associated scrutiny—they achieve this through the Local Government Finance Programme and the Local Allocation Tax.

The national government in Japan formulates the Local Government Finance Plan (LGFP) each year based on assessments and forecasts of overall revenue and expenditure in each municipality. Under this process all sources of local government revenue, including the current assignment of Local Allocation Tax as well as bonds and loans (including principal and interest payments as part of standard financial requirements), are accounted for in such a way that local government can deliver the uniform public service standard (Japanese Public Finance Fact Sheet, 2022). While the ideal situation would be for local government to cover its own expenditure via local income, in practice this is not possible due to variations in fiscal capacity. In response—using the powers of the Law Relating to the Financial Soundness of Local Governments in Japan—national government tops up revenue from the Local Allocation Tax (which is comprised of assigned portions of national taxes). A parallel Local Government Borrowing Plan provides further guidance each year and acts as a reference point for decision making, detailing how much can be borrowed and restrictions on borrowing. For example, any local governments with a debt payment ratio exceeding 17% (or those with prearranged levels) are prohibited from borrowing under the Local Government Finance Law without permission.

Sources of Income

In Japan there are at least 24 different local sources of revenue, plus others specifically created by individual local governments. This serves the purpose, compared with England, of shifting the balance of income sources from centre to locality. Local government has full control over its financial operations. However, mechanisms exist to ensure balance with central government financial operations and to secure revenue sources. The accounts of local government are classified into 'general' and 'special accounts'. General accounts are principally financed by tax revenues. Special accounts are ring-fenced for specific purposes, for example, public insurance contributions. Examples of special accounts include public enterprise accounts, national health insurance accounts, and later-stage elderly medical care accounts.

Table 7.1 describes the variety of tax available in Japan across the national and local scale.

Local income is complemented by the previously mentioned Local Allocation Tax (LAT). The LAT assigns portions of national tax—national alcohol duty, tobacco tax and income, corporate and consumption tax, providing at times 20% of local government funding. Japanese local governments also have a range of income streams associated with fixed assets, income, and consumption. The LAT is an equalising system: Tokyo Metropolis receives very little, while Akita in the north of Japan gets nearly 70% of its income from the LAT (Centre for Cities, 2019).

Table 7.1 Local and national tax in Japan

	National Taxes	Local Taxes		National Taxes	Local Taxes
Income axation	• Income tax • Corporation tax • Local corporation tax • Special corporate enterprise tax • Forest environment tax • Special income tax for reconstruction	• Inhabitant tax • Enterprise tax	Consumption taxes	• Consumption tax • Liquor tax • Tobacco tax • Special tobacco tax Gasoline tax • Local gasoline tax • Liquified petroleum gas tax • Aviation fuel tax • Petroleum and coal tax • Promotion of power resources development tax • Motor vehicle tonnage tax • International tourist tax • Tariffs • Tonnage tax • Special tonnage tax	• Local consumption tax • Local tobacco tax • Golf course utilization tax • Automobile acquisition tax • Light oil delivery tax • Automobile tax • Mine lot tax • Hunting tax • Mine production tax • Bathing tax

Asset Taxation	• Inheritance/gift tax • Registration and license tax • Stamp tax	• Real estate acquisition tax • Fixed asset tax • City planning tax • Establishment tax • Water utility and land profit tax • Common facilities tax • Housing land development tax • Special land possession tax • Discretionary tax earmarked for general use • Discretionary tax earmarked for special use • National health insurance tax

Source: Table reproduced from information in Japanese Local Government White Paper 2022 and Japan Finance Organisation for Municipalities Annual Report 2022 and Council of Local Authorities for International Relations (2022)

In addition, national treasury disbursements are also allocated to local government. This is ring-fenced funding (Bessho, 2016; Japanese Local Government White Paper, 2023). These disbursements come in three forms: national treasury obligations, grants, and payments for delegated functions. National treasury obligations are paid when there is shared responsibility between central and local government in a project, that is, central government finances the programme and local government implements it (Kameda et al., 2021). Payments for compulsory education are an example of this. Payments for 'delegated functions' are disbursements made to cover programs originally the responsibility of central government, but which were entrusted to local government for convenience and efficiency, such as election expenses for members of the National Diet (Kameda et al., 2021).

Finally, there is the possibility of (a) local bonds where the debts of local government are to be repaid over a period of time in excess of one fiscal year and (b) Bonds for Extraordinary Financial Measures, which are issued as an exception to Article 5 of the Local Finance Law to address shortages of general revenue resources of local governments (Council of Local Authorities for International Relations, 2022). Local authorities can exercise this option following consultation with the Ministry of Internal Affairs and Communications (prefectures) or the prefectural governor (municipalities). Other sources of funding include local transfer taxes, usage charges, and fees.

In the financial year of 2021, the total of local and national taxes collected amounted to 114,290.0 billion JPY. Of this 62.9% were national taxes, and the remaining 37.1% were local taxes. The latter comprised 19.7% municipal taxes and 17.4% prefectural taxes. The Local Tax Law also determines standard tax rates for local taxes on personal income, firms, fixed assets, tobacco, and consumption. Enterprise Tax and the Local Inhabitant Tax are the main local income related tax strands.[2]

[2] In practice, tax rates and ranges for local variability are set nationally. This provides a framework within which local authorities can use discretion to adjust local rates while still maintaining a degree of uniformity nationally.

The Enterprise Tax/Business Tax is a tax levied by prefectures on the taxable corporate income base, levied on value-added and capital. This is based upon measures of the business's size, such as the number of employees and amount of capital if larger than 100 million JPY. The inhabitant tax is the collective term for prefectural and municipal taxes on individual income. For individuals, there is a flat-rate component and an income-graded component which is assessed based on their income from the previous year. Corporations must pay corporate inhabitant tax to the municipalities where they have offices. These taxes are computed as a percentage of capital and business income, reflecting the financial presence and performance of the given business.

The sources of income based on fixed assets are more varied, ranging from real estate acquisition tax to national health insurance tax. For example, the fixed asset tax is an annual tax levied by municipalities on real property and depreciable fixed assets used for business purposes. Real property is taxed at 1.7% of its appraised value, while depreciable fixed assets are assessed at 1.4% of their value after statutory depreciation. In addition, the city planning tax is levied at a rate of 0.3% on land and structures within city planning zones.

Finally, local consumption tax (VAT) is imposed on goods, services, and imports in Japan at 10% (increased from 8% from October 2019). Some transactions, such as land sales, securities, and public services, are exempt from this tax. Businesses can claim credits or refunds for the consumption tax paid, subject to certain conditions. To simplify the process, an invoice system was introduced in October 2023. A lower tax rate of 8% applies to food and newspaper subscriptions, and a reverse-charge mechanism applies to cross-border digital services. 2.2% of the 10% consumption tax is allocated as local tax.

Degree of Own Budgeting and Accounting

At the prefecture level the major revenue expenditures include commerce and industry (18.3%), education (15.5%), public welfare (14.1%), debt servicing (10.6%), civil engineering work (9.5%), general administration (6.8%), sanitation (7.8%), agriculture, forestry, and fishery (3.7%%), and other (13.7%). At the municipal level, the major expenditures include public welfare (37.8%), education (11.3%), general administration (12.7%), civil engineering work (9.7%), debt servicing (8.4%), sanitation (9.6%), commerce and industry (4.5%), agriculture, forestry, and fishery (2.0%), and other (4%) (Japan Local Government Finance White Paper, 2023).

According to Japan's latest Local Finance White Paper (2022), the total revenue of local government based on the financial settlement in 2021 was 70,502.6 billion JPY, total prefectural income totalled 68,324.3 billion JPY. Local taxes are the primary sources of total annual revenue. In 2021 prefecture taxes were 32.5% of the total annual revenue for prefectures. The figure for municipalities was slightly lower at 28.7% of total annual revenue. Table 7.2 describes the composition of revenue type for prefecture and municipality while Table 7.3 breaks down local tax into its major constituent parts.

Table 7.2 Composition of local revenue

Revenue type	% of income	
	Prefecture	Municipality
Disbursements		
National Treasury Disbursement	23.7%	22.5%
Prefectural Disbursement	NA	6.5%
Special Local Grants	0.1%	0.5%
Local Allocation Tax (eEqualisation)	14.9%	13.2%
Local Taxes	32.5%	28.7%
Local Transfer Tax	2.9%	0.6%
Bonds		
Local bonds (including extraordinary measure bonds)	9.6%	7.4%
Charges, Income, and Other Sources	16.2%	20.6%
Total	100.0%	100.0%

Source: Information based on adjusted numbers from Japanese Local Government White Paper 2023

Table 7.3 Composition of local taxes

Composition of Local Taxes	
Prefecture	Municipality
Prefectural Inhabitant Tax 28.0%	Municipal Inhabitant Tax 45.7%
Local Consumption Tax 31.0 %	Fixed Asset Tax 41.4%
Enterprise Tax 25.0%	City Planning Tax 5.9%
Automobile Tax 8.1%	Municipal Tobacco Tax 3.9%
Light Oil Delivery Tax 4.7%	Other Taxes 3.1%
Real Estate Acquisition Tax 2.0%	
Prefectural Tobacco Tax 0.7%	
Other Taxes 0.5%	
Total 100.0%	Total 100.0%

Source: Information based on adjusted numbers from Japanese Local Government White Paper 2023

Method of Territorial Equalisation

In Japan, equalisation strategies to manage the disparities between different local governments are primarily comprised of national treasury disbursements and the local allocation tax. Similarly to England, the centralised disbursements are ring-fenced for specific purposes and offer local government very little discretion. The most powerful tool for equalisation is the local allocation tax (LAT). The LAT is a mechanism created to compensate for tax-raising inequalities. It guarantees that a portion of national tax revenue is used as a common financial resource for all local governments. The LAT is collected and administered by central government on behalf of local government. It is redistributed to compensate for financial imbalances and to maintain service provision—LAT-based revenue is not ring-fenced or earmarked.

The total amount of the LAT is determined in accordance with estimates of standard revenue and expenditures in local public finance as a whole. The revenue comprises fixed percentages for national taxes (33.1% for income tax and corporate tax, 50% for liquor tax, 20.8% for consumption tax, and the total amount of local corporate tax). The LAT comprises ordinary and special allocation taxes—the ordinary tax covers 94% of all payments and is used to cover financial shortfalls by respective local governments. The special allocation tax accounts for 6% of all payments and covers exceptional cases such as disasters and unique circumstances. The distribution of the LAT centres around the 'funding shortfall'—the difference between base financial needs and revenue. Financial needs are calculated with a prescribed formula for each administrative cost, such as civil engineering or education costs, to measure the financial needs of an authority. The calculation begins with the cost to maintain services in a standard entity, and is adjusted based on population, area, and unique regional circumstances, to determine each entity's specific base financial need (Council of Local Authorities for International Relations, 2022).

The base revenue amount is 75% of the estimated standard revenue for prefectures and municipalities, as extrapolated from recently collected tax revenue. The percentage is not 100% to avoid discouraging local government from increasing local taxes. This is because if the ordinary allocation tax is reduced by the same amount as any increase in local tax revenue, local governments that increased local taxes would not receive additional revenue overall. If the total revenue shortfall for a local government is less than the ordinary allocation tax amount, the shortfall is adjusted to match the ordinary allocation tax amount. Negligible distribution is made to areas such as Tokyo, whose base revenues far exceed their financial needs. These are known as 'non-receiving entities' and are a net contributor into the overall local government finance system in Japan. In the eventuality that LAT does not fully cover the total funding shortfall of a local government, central government can implement local financing measures, including allowing the borrowing of additional funds or transfers from the general account (special fund transfers) to the LAT special account.

Summary

The following observations can be made about the Japanese local government finance system, as it relates to the potential for change in England:

- Japanese local government finance is again an example of an adaptive system, one that has only recently been reformed in order to embed greater local autonomy and overall financial resilience. Transition to financial resilience, via the 'Trinity Reform' initiated in the early 2000s, provides a reference point for how a system heavily criticised for its centralised tendencies, and agency approach to local government, can reform relatively quickly. The underlying rationale of the 'Trinity Reform' was the belief that one of the central root causes of severe local government financial distress lay in the weak capacity of local government to generate and/or have discretion over its own tax revenue and income. There was an acceptance that decentralised decision making was a key feature of well-functioning and resilient local government finance systems. Creating distributed problem-solving capacity leads to resilience from disruptions because the system can adapt at the local level to unexpected changes and reduce the chance of system-wide failure.
- While decentralisation and autonomy feature heavily in the constitution and related legislation, the system of sub-national government is very heterogeneous, and is thus able to meet specific local requirements. It is important to note that the priority accorded to autonomy is part of a wider embedded system of intergovernmental financial relations and scrutiny. This is a recognised feature of efficient adaptive systems, where positive feedback loops (in this case local decision-making autonomy) amplify the potential for innovation and adaptive capacity which are then counter-balanced by negative feedback loops (in this case, the constraining effects of scrutiny and oversight) that play a critical role in system stability and overall balance. Negative feedback loops counterbalance any deviation from perceived system equilibrium—an example in the Japanese case is the proactive process of insolvency prevention.

- Like Germany and Italy, Japanese municipal revenue is much more diverse than England with prefectures and municipalities benefiting from more than 20 local taxes, alongside national treasury disbursements. This creates a varied revenue base upon which to make decisions and creates considerable levels of system redundancy as local authorities are not reliant on single financial instruments. In England, there is often a zero-sum debate between central allocation and fiscal devolution, in which all viable changes consist of more of one and less of the other. The Japanese system demonstrates that national treasury disbursements (equivalents of which also exist in England) can exist alongside assigned revenue and locally sourced income in a coherent system.
- In Japan there is a systematic assessment of relative needs and available income which includes costs associated with debt management. Where there is shortfall in income at the local level, to cover expenditure, the LAT is adjusted to compensate. This financial relationship minimises the risk of unfunded mandates and guarantees the delivery of minimum service levels. In this sense the operation of the LAT dampens system-based inequality and ensures that the overall Japanese local government finance system maintains the ability to operate consistently.
- In parallel with the Trinity Reform, since the enactment of the Law Relating to the Financial Soundness of Local Governments, the number of local governments needing improvement measures has reduced markedly, with only a very small minority under either red or yellow card status. Enhanced financial reporting, early warning signals, and improvement plans are now a proactive part of the local government finance system in Japan, targeting even the smallest signs of distress.
- This targeted process provides an important benchmark for turnaround management (Stevens, 2013) and a set of lessons for the development of a scrutiny system that could (a) help counter the increasing number of section 114 notices in England and (b) provide reassurance to central government that decentralisation can work hand in hand with an embedded process of system-based scrutiny. In addition, while a 'red card' system could tackle those local authorities in most distress, a 'yellow card' system could reveal the potentially much bigger problem of those local authorities who are just about solvent but exist on

the permanent margin of viability and face increasingly constrained ability to deliver public services.

- In addition to the thriving number of intergovernmental associations, the Local Autonomy Act defines the relationship between national and local government and provides an objective foundation for any dispute between the respective tiers of government. There is also a Local Autonomy Committee (Chihou Jichi Chousaki) hosted by the Ministry of Internal Affairs and Communications. This committee investigates (via referral) disputes between local government and the state, providing a forum for their resolution.
- Like many other countries Japan faces the challenge of how to balance the incentivisation of local economic activity through decentralisation of tax and redistribution of income between rich and poor locations. Japan achieves this through national treasury allocations, assignment of major national taxes, the LAT, and a diverse array of local tax options. This provides a case example of a more discretionary and resilient local government financial system. Inequality can undermine the resilience of the local government system by creating social tensions and reducing the capacity of less well-resourced local authorities to adapt to change.
- It is important to note that devolution is not a panacea for all of the challenges of local government. Respondents made clear that while devolution and decentralisation are important facets of local government finance in Japan, when tasks are devolved in isolation or in excessive quantum, they can place too much burden on prefectures and municipalities. Rather, echoing the whole system approach advocated in this study, respondents indicated that tasks need to be assigned and funded at the appropriate tier of government.

References

Bessho, S.-I. (2016). *Case study of central and local government finance in Japan*. Asian Development Bank Institute.

Centre for Cities. (2019). *What does Japan tell us about the potential for fiscal devolution?* Centre for Cities.

Council of Local Authorities for International Relations. (2022). *Local government in Japan 2020.* 2022 Revised Edition.

Hirota, H., & Yunoue, H. (2022). Fiscal rules and creative accounting: Evidence from Japanese municipalities. *Journal of the Japanese and International Economies, 63*, 101172. https://doi.org/10.1016/j.jjie.2021.101172

Japanese Ministry of Finance. (2023). *White paper on local government finance: Fact sheet.* Japanese Government.

Kameda, T., Namba, R., & Tsuruga, T. (2021). Decomposing local fiscal multipliers: Evidence from Japan. *Japan and the World Economy, 57*, 101053. https://doi.org/10.1016/j.japwor.2021.101053

Machidori, S. (2023). *Decentralisation reforms, in: Political reform reconsidered: The trajectory of a transformed Japanese state.* Springer.

OECD. (2022). *World observatory on subnational government finance and investment—Japan.* Retrieved 23, June 2023, from https://www.sng-wofi.org/country-profiles/

Seaton, P. (2010). Depopulation and financial collapse in Yabari: Market forces, administrative folly, or a warning to others? *Social Science Japan Journal, 13*(2), 227–240. https://doi.org/10.1093/ssjj/jyp045

Stevens, A. (2013, July 31). *Japanese city's financial collapse offers a number of interesting lessons.*

8

Reform in England: What if Local Government was Funded Differently in England

International Summary

England is not alone in facing local government finance pressures. All three international locations face financial pressure and also territorial divergence in the make-up and quantity of revenue sources and spending pressure. In particular, all three locations are struggling to fund the increasing costs of health and social care, while protecting more discretionary spending imperatives associated with local place. In addition, all three locations are still heavily dependent on central transfers and uneven development is present in all three locations. Ring-fenced income is substantially present in each system.

Common elements in each case study that are absent from England include regular relative needs assessments and consequent processes of equalisation between location; flexible and varied forms of inter-territorial government; a comprehensive and transparent system of financial regulation; formal structures for discussion and negotiation between tiers of government, alongside associations of local authorities; and a much broader basket of local income sources. These latter points, in relation to revenue sources, make for local government finance systems that are

K. Muldoon-Smith et al., *Embedded Autonomy*,
https://doi.org/10.1007/978-981-97-9030-2_8

significantly less reliant on territorially specific local property tax, and instead more connected to income and economic productivity. Ring-fenced revenue is mostly confined to 'agency functions', carried out by local authorities on behalf of central government, or for funds related to a crisis event such as Covid-19, or disaster management.

Local government autonomy and resilience is institutionally embedded in all three locations. Forms of subsidiarity, solidarity, connexity, and equivalence underpin all three systems, mitigating against the emergence of unfunded mandates, and creating a constitutional principle of symmetry between revenue and expenditure. In each country, the state ensures adequate total financing (vertical equalisation) and individual locations with more income support those with less income (horizontal equalisation). At the same time, all locations are reducing their debt burden and are following some form of minimum debt ratio alongside balanced budget principles. All three locations have also brought in fiscal oversight to ward off local authority insolvency: The Stability Council and debt commissioners in Germany, Article 244 of the TUEL in Italy, and the traffic light system associated with the Yubari insolvency in Japan. These two features—adequate financing and transparent oversight systems—cannot be viewed in isolation. Adequate financing implies a core governance role for local authorities which deserves oversight; local authorities can accept stronger oversight because they are secure within the overall governance system. In England, these two system features are, so to speak, stranded on opposite sides of an adversarial debate between central and local government.

In terms of capital spending, there is less debate around local authority debt and commercial investment—in Italy there is even the threat of a debt ban if a local authority does not deliver a balanced budget. In some respects, the situation England now finds itself in, featuring fiscal gaps and in certain cases flirtation with borrowing and debt, is similar to that seen in these locations in the 2000s and early 2010s. For example, Germany used a version of the exceptional financial measures currently being adopted in England during this period. However, the historical application of debt to fill short-term budget gaps is now regarded as an explicit indicator of fiscal distress in Germany, rather than a viable tool for balancing local government budgets.

Moreover, echoing the managerialism of new public management, and perhaps inviting the ire of those arguing for devolution in England, it is clear that performance management and scrutiny form a necessary part of a resilient local government finance system. In England, the momentum around devolution and local autonomy has coincided with a suspicion towards methods of performance management and comprehensive review. Such approaches are seen as an extension of the state in its attempt to control and discipline local authorities. One of our central findings is that this antipathy does not exist internationally, with scrutiny and oversight seen as a helpful component of a well-functioning local government finance system. In all three locations, local autonomy and discretion is complemented by a methodical process of monitoring and scrutiny to maintain overall system resilience. This presents a trade-off between autonomy and resilience which is managed by constitutional courts, conferences, and autonomy committees. The stated role of local government and its underpinning principles forms an important reference point. The fact that, in all three locations, the approach and demands of local government are justiciable via constitutional courts is an important cornerstone, but not the only part, of this relationship.

Complementing this situation, the system of audit in each country has a more interactive relationship with local government. For example, the audit institutions in Italy have a role in the constitution, influencing local government fiscal policy and the planning of any corrective action. They play both a consultive and jurisdictional function as a constitutional body. This helps to balance the constitutional emphasis on autonomy of local government with the requirements of central coordination, oversight, and overall financial resilience.

In short, all three case study locations have a clear set of coordinates that detail their role and function. This then forms the basis for relative needs assessment and consequent financial arrangements. All three locations also have either explicit or stated intentions to provide minimum service levels.[1] Local autonomy and financial resilience is built into the German Basic Law. It affords local government the right to

[1] In Italy this is still controversial, with considerable delay in finalising and publishing the minimum service levels.

self-administration through the principle of republicanism (Article 20); thus, each local government has the power to determine its own constitutional mandate to manage its affairs. As a federal republic, local and central levels of government share power as equal stakeholders through a written constitution (Geissler et al., 2021). Amendments to the constitution must be approved by both levels of government, meaning that the subnational level cannot be abolished nor have their powers unilaterally altered by the central tier of government. In Italy, the same principles are built into the amended 2001 Constitution—sub-national governments were given the same status as national government. Specifically, Article 119 recognised financial autonomy for local government and Article 120 laid down the basis for proportionate finance. This Framework Law of 2009 hardwired fiscal federalism into administrative procedures between central, regional, and local government. Like Germany, it is essentially a codified constitutional provision, setting out the respective roles for different tiers of government. The result is that each region, and municipality, has the discretion to determine its own constitutional mandate. This is being pushed even further with the increasingly recognised movement towards differentiated autonomy prioritised by the northern regions.

The path towards the creation of resilient local government finance systems has not been linear in each country. Local autonomy is a long-held facet of German territorial governance. The principles of local government autonomy and resilience were founded upon the German Basic Law in the late 1940s. This path has been more recent in Italy while in Japan it has slowly developed since the 1940s, with momentum building over a number of years. While the role of local government is set out in the German and Italian constitution, in Japan it is not set out in the constitution: the Local Autonomy Law and Omnibus Local Autonomy Law sets out the specific role of local government alongside the momentum created by the Trinity Reforms in the early 2000s. In each case, this forms the cornerstone for the basic operation of local government—outlining matters such as types, powers, legislative assemblies, agencies, and financial affairs. These fixed coordinates also outline the vertical intergovernmental relationship between state and local government and the horizontal relationship between respective local governments. While all three locations are considerable resources for understanding the functions of a resilient local government finance system, the evolution in Japan perhaps has the greatest similarity to the challenge currently faced in England. Japan has deliberately moved from a system of centralisation and local agency function to one based on local autonomy through a process of legislation rather than constitutional change—while also tackling insolvent local governments.

In this chapter, we apply these findings to the situation in England. First, we set out some proposals for reform in England and then, building on the various transition processes seen overseas, we consider how change could be managed in England.

Those calling for reform or making suggestions for changes to the local government finance system often encounter a range of defensive responses:

- Our ways of doing things date back many hundreds of years, why would we change them?
- The system is simply too complicated to fix.
- Reform in the system, particularly the assignment of big-ticket income sources, will prove too costly.
- We need to protect taxpayers' money from local government inefficiency and balance the yearly budget.
- This is dangerous!—the fallout from the community charge in the early 1990s still looms large in the UK government's collective psyche.

To engage with these concerns, we start from the vantage point of how change could happen and what would it look like within what appears to be a critical juncture of change in the mode of governance in England. Our proposals have been developed mindful of key characteristics of the UK's short- to medium-term political context. First, *money* is in short supply—and 'new taxes' are always unpopular—so the proposals focus on the more effective use of existing funds. Second, moving from a top-down central–local relationship to a more partnership-based polity is a large and unfamiliar step for the British political system. New sources of funding will generate effects across the local government system: for this type of change to endure, those effects must be acknowledged and managed. This calls for consensus and trust and cautions against wholesale change in the short term.

Consequently, the following six proposals set out how the international findings could be applied to England. The proposals are presented chronologically and in order of logical implementation. These proposals are:

- Stabilise the existing local government finance system.
- Rework the local government needs assessment [the Fair Funding Review].
- Establish a systematic form of territorial equalisation between local authorities.
- Establish a proactive model for assessing local authority financial health and financial management.
- Establish a standing commission, akin to the 'English Devolution Council' proposed by the Institute for Government.
- Develop a long-term programme of local tax reform and exploration of assigning national tax revenues to local authorities.

Stabilise the System

Before considering any reform of local government finance in England, it is important to take immediate steps to stabilise the existing system. This is in order to safeguard the short-term prospects for local government but also to create time to consider the wider reform of local government finance. For instance, learning from the international locations' experience with debt, it is important that efforts towards immediate stabilisation go beyond the current process of 'exceptional financial support'. As already argued, these measures risk storing up debt burdens in the medium to long term—the presence of such measures overseas is now a specific indicator of financial distress in these locations.

The pragmatic way of doing this, and perhaps the most immediately powerful, is to increase certainty within the local government budgeting process. Local councils need to know how much funding they will get in 2025–2026 and perhaps 2026–2027 at the very least. It is clear in the research that councils understand the economic and administrative realities of the largely insolvent public finance system. They understand reform will not come quickly if it is going to be ambitious, but they need the ability to plan while this reform process takes place.

This argues for a definite commitment to a root-and-branch reform of the financing system to be implemented before the end of the 2024–2029 parliament. In the shorter term, the funding settlement for 2025–2026 should include genuine consultation between tiers of government to pick up issues and adjust funding. Any stabilisation and reform programme may not be welcomed by all local authorities, reflecting the winners and losers in any given situation. For example, some local authorises may be sitting on a significant quantity of retained business rates that would be redistributed under any reset. Councils in this position may argue that they have limited bandwidth to consider reform while coming to terms with a new Government and associated policy objectives.

It is clear from international findings that stabilisation should be considered in tandem with reform, not sequentially—as any immediate injection of new funds will only be a sticking plaster solution that disguises the impossible situation that the majority of local authorities find themselves in—rewarding short term tactical decisions over medium to longer term thinking. The longer reform is delayed, the more unstable the overall local government finance system becomes. Additional funds allocated under out-of-date formulas and needs assessments only increase imbalances of funding between locations—and thus each annual financial settlement makes substantial reform harder to deliver.

That being said, at the time of writing, immediately after Labour winning the general election in early July 2024, there is not enough time to consider a multi-year funding settlement. Spending plans need to be completed by November 2024 and multi-year settlements take time to complete. It would be prudent to propose a one-year spending review following the election, with a multi-year spending review and reform package from 2026–2027: at the time of writing, it appears that this timetable is the Government's plan. There is a tension between providing councils with clear multiyear allocations immediately, and the time needed to devise them in such a way that a new government can embed its new policy priorities. The focus should be on creating a new funding structure that does not need immediate revisions in subsequent years.

What Would This Achieve in England?

- Stabilisation would create space for both local and central government to consider the local government finance situation. Jointly considering these perspectives begins the work of restoring trust between the two 'sides'.
- This will enable local authorities to consider their position and for central government to consider their position between the recent general election result and the likely spending reviews or equivalent on the horizon.
- With reform in mind, central government will be able to consider the time, effort, financial cost, and political capital involved in setting out any priorities for reform.
- Enhanced certainty, created by longer budget projects for local government, will enable the sector to plan resources in the short to medium term.

Assessing the Relative Needs of the Local Government Finance System

Germany, Italy, and Japan all have a mature and detailed process of relative needs assessment. In England, needs assessment has been suspended since the introduction of business rate retention in 2013. This system was designed to include regular 'resets', where needs would be reassessed, but these have not taken place so far. The Government launched a 'fair funding review' in 2016, but this has not progressed since a consultation in 2018, nor has the model of local business rate retention been reset, as originally envisioned. The fair funding review would have reassessed a range of indicators of local need and taken decisions about the relative weighting of those indicators. Not doing so has left considerable mismatch between local need and resource and also between location (Institute for Fiscal Studies, 2023).

If this process were completed, it would lay the ground for redistributing funds between local authorities more closely in line with an assessment of need (see next section). As things stand, the dynamics of the business rate retention scheme would mean that funding would then diverge from the needs assessment over time, in line with local rate revenues, pending a further needs assessment in the future. The reach of the Fair Funding Review (or a similar comprehensive public finance exercise) could be extended to apply it to specific grants within the Local Government Finance Settlement (LGFS) as well as (Revenue Support Grant) RSG/(Settlement Funding Assessment (SFA). Those specific grants totalled £7855m in 2023–2024: RSG is £1905m. The general grants listed in the local growth and place fund register, published by DLUHC in 2023, could also be included. They would add a further £3.5bn per year to the total funding available. That decision would be in line with the new government's intention largely to end competitive bidding programmes for local authorities.

These changes would immediately address the current situation of unfunded mandates and bring England more closely into line with best practice overseas. While it is important to consider the relative needs of each location, it is also important to consider the efficiency of this exercise. While considering a new needs assessment, it would be possible to simplify the range of indicators used substantially, and to simplify the needs assessment's 'four-block model' (see LG Futures, 2017). This would go a considerable way to simplifying the funding system and making it more transparent and related to relative need between local authorities.

What Would This Achieve in England?

- This change would substantially reduce ring-fencing and competitive bid culture, consolidating all or most funding into a single amount.
- It would remove most of the bureaucratic overhead on local authorities required to account separately for spending funding sources. The fragmentation of the local government finance system and the short-term and uncertain nature of grant funding is a considerable drain on local authority resources during an era of considerable staff reduction.

- It would remove the counter-intuitive incentive for cash-poor authorities to apply for funding for projects that do not reflect their requirements, as they would have greater latitude over the use of funds.
- It would ensure that funding better reflected changes in population and need between authorities since 2013. Including additional funds in the scope of the needs assessment would help to smooth the impact of these changes on individual authorities.

Ensuring Fair Territorial Equalisation

While all of the locations in this study face considerable pressure upon their public finances, England is an outlier in not having a systematic form of solidarity-based territorial equalisation, which ensures parity in needs-based revenue between location. Germany, Italy, and Japan all utilise forms of vertical (central to local) and horizontal (between location) redistributions of major income streams (including elements of personal, company, consumption, and asset taxes) that ensure that all locations have access to resources. These equalisation systems are the basic means of making sure that all local authorities have access to resources and is the practical implementation of the underlying principles of solidarity found in all three countries—for example, the Solidarity Fund in Italy. Relative needs assessment is the first foundation stone in a reformed local government finance system—it assesses in relative terms what local authorities actually need.

However, it is inevitable that this exercise will reveal mismatches between relative need and resource and, consequently, there is a subsequent need to redistribute income to ensure a resilient local government finance system based on equity. Exposing these mismatches is a risk factor whenever a system of funding distribution remains un-revised for a substantial number of years. Individual authorities become accustomed to their funding allocations and build medium-term strategies around them, and they will inevitably protest if they stand to lose out from a reform. Amalgamating the various sources of existing funding noted above into a single allocation, and broad consultation on the approach to distribution, may mitigate that threat to some extent. The English system has in the past used 'damping' to this end—capping the degree of change to distribution outcomes from one financial year to the next.

What Would This Achieve in England?

- Alongside efficient financial management, a system of equalisation based on sound needs assessment would help remove the risk of increased Section 114 notices. In particular, it would help to give local authorities more certainty in their budget position which will give more room for manoeuvre and allow for future planning.
- It is important that the system of equalisation is not ring-fenced—the funding within the equalisation systems in the international locations is not ring-fenced and this results in individual local authorities having significant discretion over large quantities of income. Such a system of equalisation recognises that all locations do not have access to buoyant local income streams and opens the door to all locations being able to take part in devolution and some form of local decision-making and accountability.
- This is the essence of embedded autonomy—fiscal autonomy is not a panacea for resilient local government finance, although it is often taken as an article of faith in the England debate. Without equalisation, autonomy only benefits those locations with buoyant income streams and relatively low demands upon service.

Establish a Proactive Model for Assessing Local Authority Financial Health

A central finding in this research is that resilient local government finance systems with local discretion operate in tandem with proactive methods of monitoring financial distress and performance. All three locations have positive notions of scrutiny hardwired into their local government finance systems and recognise it as a positive means of ensuring a resilient local government system—echoing the recommendations in the Redmond Review (2020) for a reform of local audit. This recognises that local government is inherently complex and riven with short-, medium-, and long-term pressures. It also recognises that any system with in-built discretion and autonomy will inevitably lead to enhanced territorial divergence in outcome and approach. Monitoring of financial health and performance lays the foundations for maintaining overall system stability and certainty, managing the trade-off between autonomy and resilience. There is potential to streamline and aggregate existing reporting of local authority financial returns in the manner of the five indicators in the Japanese local authority finance early warning system.

In parallel with this process and learning from the debt brake in Germany and the golden rule principle in Italy, all three locations have taken steps to manage and then reduce their exposure to debt. The debt brake in Germany limits any borrowing to a proportion of GDP, while the golden rule principle states that local authorities can only take out new loans and other sources of financing if the annual amount of related interest, in addition to the charges already in place (loans previously contracted, bonds previously issued, credit openings stipulated and guarantees given, net of state and regional interest subsidies), do not exceed a pre-determined level of current revenue. We propose that the same rules should be followed in England—but in tandem with removing ring-fencing of funding and avoiding unfunded mandates.

What Would This Achieve in England?

- Recognising that section 114 notices are likely to increase in quantum in the short to medium term, a traffic light system modelled on the early warning system in Japan would help to proactively monitor and manage local authorities at risk of issuing section 114 notices (red card local authorities).
- It would also take account of the far larger quantity of local authorities currently at the margins of viability, those struggling to balance their budgets, utilising their reserves, and, at the upper extremes, those in receipt of 'exceptional financial support' measures (yellow card local authorities).
- More positively it would also recognise those local authorities who are continuing to operate with balanced budgets and significant reserves (green card local authorities).
- Not only would this help highlight the relative financial health of local authority finances, it would also help recognise that *financial health* is a systemic component of intergovernmental working and fiscal transfer,

moving away from the atomistic approach of dealing with insolvency after the event and treating it as arising purely from local circumstances.
- Debt management rules and limitation would prevent borrowing becoming a systemic part of the local government finance system in England. In Japan, Germany, and Italy, extensive income from shared and local taxes is complemented by confirmation of local budgets and voluntary restrictions on borrowing. This would provide reassurance to the Treasury that a more flexible system of finance could be scrutinised.

The monitoring of local authority financial health would be complemented by a move towards a light-touch system of assessing local government performance against outcomes. This system would consist of a small number of sophisticated and clearly thought-out outcome metrics. The system could be operated by an independent iteration of the new Office for Local Government (OFLOG). To maximise trust in this assessment, OFLOG could be legally reconstituted as an independent body, reporting to Parliament. It would work alongside the financial health traffic light system and function as an early warning system for local authority financial and delivery failure.

What Would This Achieve in England?

This change would serve as a rebooting of the central–local relationship in England, which has been dogged by conflict in recent decades. The Italian local government finance system operates a similar system which is, in part, based on the Comprehensive Performance Assessment deployed in England in the early 2000s.

- In the international locations, this type of assessment is managed by an independent body (typically a 'court of accounts' or constitutional court), not by the central government. In the vast majority of cases the assessment is a formality.
- This type of process could be expected to pick up, for instance, the misallocation of minimum revenue provision within local authority budgets, which has featured in a number of local authorities' decisions to issue a section 114 notice in the early 2020s.

Establish an Inter-territorial Standing Commission

All locations recognise that alongside scrutiny, meaningful inter-governmental communication and negotiation is central to maintaining local government finance autonomy and resilience. An inter-territorial standing commission would provide a one-stop, regular discussion forum for local authority representatives and the Government. The UK Government established three new local-national bodies in late 2024: a Council of the Nations and Regions, a Mayors' Council, and a (local authority) Leaders' Council. The Council of the Nations and Regions is to facilitate engagement and collaboration on 'cross-cutting challenges': no terms of reference have been published for the other two bodies at the time of writing. The standing commission proposed here is a different type of body. It would be a pro-active vehicle for consultation on government proposals, raising of emerging issues, negotiation of financial agreements, and mediation of conflict. This would form an essential pillar of a more developed settlement, or concordat between local and national government. The commission would provide local government with a voice in public finance but also help central government understand what local government wants.

In shaping any reform of local government finance, it is also important to consider what central government thinks of the local government sector, and the struggle central government has to understand the often fragmented and contradictory demands of the local state. Local government finance is an interaction between the central and local state, and in renewing the finance system, it is imperative that central government understands clearly what local government wants in order to strengthen the system.

Central governments typically view local governments through a lens of balancing autonomy and oversight, aiming to ensure national coherence while respecting local governance. English local government is currently seen as an agent for delivering national policy at the local level, rather than creators of their own policy and makers of their own decisions. This constrained agent model of working can be understood within some of the long-held concerns that the UK government holds towards local government. Reflex concerns exist regarding the capacity and competence of local authorities to effectively carry out their responsibilities, but also various fears associated with what might happen to the sector if the type of reform presented in this book is put into action. For example, might autonomous local governments pursue different interpretations of national policies or reject them altogether, leading to fragmentation, inefficiency, and conflict with national objectives? Embedded autonomy acknowledges this concern and looks to counter it via effective coordination with the local government sector and oversight.

The standing commission should be underwritten by a concordat that sets the points of reference and role for the standing commission and backed by statutory status. This will avoid the risk of the commission being ignored or passed over in favour of other priorities. Scotland's recent Verity House Agreement (published in 2023) provides an interesting example close to home of a memorandum of understanding between local and central government that supports many of the principles advocated for in this book, but it was inhibited by its lack of legal standing. The Scottish Government went on almost immediately to ignore it in 2024, freezing council tax without consultation with local authorities.

The Central-Local Concordat of 2007, agreed between the Government of the day and the Local Government Association (LGA), provides a sound initial foundation for the development of an inter-territorial standing commission. The agreement referred to the European Charter of Self Government and committed central and local government to work together giving people a clearer understanding of what public money is spent in their area, and towards giving councils greater flexibility in their funding.

It is envisioned that the proposed standing commission would be chaired by an independent OFLOG, supported by an expert advisory group to advise on local government finance practice, helping define objectives and understanding the impact of delivery and legislation. The commission would need to include stakeholders from the county, metropolitan, and combined authorities as well as associations representing local authorities and the relevant Secretary of State and his or her ministerial team. The commission would operate and make recommendations in its own right, underpinned by a revised concordat and backed by its statutory role and status.

What Would This Achieve in England?

- Germany, Italy, and Japan all have comparable institutions that are politically neutral, well-resourced, embedded, and respected. Such institutions practise intergovernmental coordination and strengthen relationships between the respective tiers of government.
- As with the UK's intergovernmental relations machinery, a possible structure would be a main forum complemented by a series of subject committees, which would include attendance from a broad range of government departments.
- There is significant demand throughout the sector for a formalised approach to the representation of local government in national policy and structured dialogue between local and national policy makers. Equally, it would provide a ready route for central government departments to co-ordinate with local authorities and avoid misunderstandings and tensions.
- The commission would provide a forum for central departments and public bodies looking to engage with localities and/or with the sector in order to design and implement policy.
- The commission would provide a forum to discuss matters such as local taxation, grants and needs assessment, and financial management. It could debate and formally or informally sign off a new needs assessment approach.
- The commission would be likely to save resources by applying expertise to emerging (and emergency) policy. Subjects covered need not be restricted to local government responsibilities: they might include, for instance, matters such as water, immigration pressures, and health services.

Develop a Long-term Programme to Explore Tax Reform

Alongside reduced ring-fencing of income, a notable component of all three locations was the access to more varied local taxes and also the assignment of big-ticket national revenue streams. This broadens the debate from a narrow focus on 'fiscal devolution'. A wide range of taxes have been slated for transfer to local government, but these are often peripheral in revenue terms and/or vary widely in their incidence between locations (Muldoon-Smith & Sandford, 2021). We propose a fixed percentage of the revenue from one or more national taxes would be assigned to local government as a whole. Revenue could be assigned from one or more of income tax, VAT, employers' national insurance, corporation tax, vehicle excise duty, and stamp duty. It would take some time to design a system that was accepted by stakeholders, and to introduce the administrative capacity to implement it: therefore this change should come after the initial stabilisation of the system proposed above.

Providing additional sources of local authority revenue could open space for debate around reforming council tax and business rates. It is notable that all three case study locations have recently gone through various forms of residential and commercial property tax reform. In all three cases, property taxes are considerably lower than in the UK, and therefore make up a smaller proportion of local authority revenues: it is likely that reforms to them would be less politically charged as a result. Council tax (domestic property tax) is based on property valuations from 1991, and is relatively regressive, being based on eight bands rather than individual property values. Business rates (non-domestic property tax) normally take no account of economic performance, unlike local taxes in the three case studies. English local government's reliance on these property taxes for revenue causes the local authority financial system to be dependent on the uncertain future dynamics of residential and commercial property. There is currently considerable uncertainty in relation to how much commercial property businesses need in an era of hybrid working. Any reduction in floor space would have the knock-on impacts for the quantum of tax collection. As a result, there is scope to learn from the international locations and incorporate an element of business turnover or profit into the current formulation of business rates to capture the bricks and mortar and performance elements of business. The new UK government issued a consultation in late 2024 on proposals to introduce additional multipliers for retail and large businesses, indicating an interest in the scope to adjust local taxation to address concerns around local economic buoyancy.

Shared taxes could be distributed according to the needs assessment proposed above. Areas could, alternatively, be permitted to keep a proportion of increased revenue against a baseline, in the manner of business rate retention. However, the role of revenue incentives should not be overplayed: there is little evidence that it plays much role in our international case studies while it tends to reward already buoyant economies in England.

What Would This Achieve in England?

- Access to a more varied basket of local income sources would acknowledge that the demands for 'more taxes for local government' often focus on options (e.g., tourism tax) that attract minor amounts of extra revenue.
- It would also acknowledge that English local authorities' range of local revenue sources is limited compared with other countries, with comparative over-reliance on property taxes that have long operated at the boundary of legitimacy (due to high rates and increasingly complex methods of valuation).
- Assigning national tax revenues has the benefit of not (necessarily) comprising 'new taxes' or 'increasing taxes' at the local level. For example, in Germany, localities receive shares of national income tax and VAT revenues, but they do not have powers to raise an additional rate.
- Assigning national taxes to the local authorities also prevents an over-reliance on local sources of revenue, which can be cyclical and uneven between location.
- There have been significant calls for flexibility in relation to local tax rates to help manage local finance and potential economic growth. However, the findings in all three locations suggest that local authorities rarely use these powers (even when they have the ability to do so). Moreover, the international locations indicate those that do take the opportunity to do so are likely to be those local authorities in financial distress desperately trying to raise revenue—the inadvertent consequence is businesses can be incentivised to leave for lower tax rates elsewhere.

- While there has been some debate around new methods of taxing property—for example various modes of land value tax—property taxes featured far less in the case studies than in England and far greater impact could be achieved by assigning bigger ticket VAT and income taxes. Access to a broader basket of taxes would open the potential for more discretion at the local level. It is likely that sharing tax revenues would be complemented by a reduction in transfer grants—as was the case when the Business Rate Retention Scheme was established—and thus this would not constitute a bald proposal for 'more cash'.
- Access to substantial and sustained sums of money would increase local government resilience. Predictable revenue levels would enable local authorities to plan long-term with greater confidence. This will be a substantial gain in an environment where financial strain has been the norm for many years. Sustainable finance is a necessary condition for confident and resilient local public service provision.
- The system can be future proofed to allow for some degree of incentivisation for local authorities to improve economic conditions and benefit from increased revenues–and/or for additional local tax rates to be charged—establishing the joint principles that local government is a part of the national delivery of public services, but that it also has an independent democratic mandate at the local level.
- Establishing and agreeing any system would take the bulk of a parliamentary term after consultation and legislation. A first parliamentary term could be used to advocate and bed in the concept.

Adapting the capital stack model seen in real estate development, Fig. 8.1 envisions what this new local income approach could look like in England. A capital stack represents the layered resources that go into a real estate purchase or a property development. For example, the mix of equity and debt, and the order that each would be applied and redeemed in a given scheme. In recent years, the same principles have been applied in the urban context to understand the potential for attracting and financing urban development schemes and the development of an investment playbook (Katz & Bradley, 2013). We take this approach one step further to capture the income resources that could be available to local authorities in England after reform.

Local Revenue					
	National taxes	**Local taxes**		**National taxes**	**Local taxes**
Income taxation *	• Income tax • National insurance contribution (NUC) tax • Corporation tax	• Business turnover tax (new component of business rates) • Assignment of income tax, NIC and corporation tax (portion of that collected nationally)	Consumption taxes	• Consumption tax • Vehicle excise duty • Excise tax (alcohol, tobacco, gambling, petrol)	• Assignment of comsumption tax • Tourist tax • Environmental zone tax • Assignment of vehicle excise duty
Asset taxation*	• Inheritance/gift tax • Capital gains tax • Stamp duty tax	• Business rates (property component). • Council tax • Assignment of capital gains tax • Assignment of stamp duty tax			
Local charges	Charges and fees for services				

Local capital finance and borrowing		
Local authority and partner equity	Debt	The lending or partnership vehicle – this can be a standard debt vehicle via PWLB or a more complex arrangement between partners – for example lease back or property wrap agreements.

Government transfers			
Capital transfers: to pay for large infrastructure projects such as transport and net zero retrofit strategies. This would still be ring fenced.	**Incentive grants:** to pay for government and political projects. This should be minimised to remove complexity and ambiguity in the overall government system.	**Shared function payments:** to pay for services/responsibilities that are shared between central and local government. For example, health and education. This would still be ring -fenced.	**General solidarity grant:** based on a relative needs assessment, this national grant system will retain overall balance and solvency in the local government finance system. It will not be ring fenced.
Territorial Equalisation: In conjunction with the general solidarity fund this mechanism and the existing business rate retention scheme will ensure that all local authorities are adequately financed.			
*Selected list			

Fig. 8.1 Proposed local income stack in England

The local income stack presents a broader appreciation of the income sources potentially available to local authorities and consequently the decisions they could make if they were provided with more discretion and control over more income sources. While the capital stack model fixes on capital and the potential for investment in local areas (and potential financialisation), the local income stack incorporates capital and revenue funding as well as methods of redistribution and central government support. Read from the bottom up, it first considers equalisation and central transfers. It then considers the use of local authority equity and capital financing strategies before detailing the potential assignment of national taxes to local areas, alongside existing local taxes and charges. It is important to note that in this income stack conceptualisation, local government transfers are not the dominant mode of funding. Rather, they hold the balance in funding and contribute to equalisation after all other income sources have been considered.

Summary

Inevitably, all of these proposals cannot be delivered at once. They are presented in pragmatic order. Stabilisation and the parallel re-working of the needs assessment logically come first, to acknowledge changes in local demands upon finance and available resource. This would operate in tandem with an efficient means of territorial equalisation and the development of a standing commission to manage, in collaborative fashion, the relationship between scales of government and related interests. In parallel, a longer-term programme would explore the assignment of national tax revenues to local authorities. Inspiration can be taken from the Trinity Reform in Japan during the early 2000s that laid out the legislative framework for reworking the Japanese local government finance system around principles of sub-national financing. Taken together, these principles indicate how financial resilience and meaningful discretion, and autonomy can be embedded in local government working.

Why have these mechanisms either not been put into action, and how can meaningful transition be accelerated? The next chapter considers this situation through the lens of complex system thinking and embedded autonomy. First of all, it considers the long held and 'sticky' institutional environment and settled mechanisms that stymie local government finance reform and the long-held instinct to control from the centre. Then, learning from the international case studies, it assesses how the English local government finance system can transition into a new way of working and provide the basis for a revived local government sector. It argues that policy and regulatory approaches that focus on specific aspects of local government finance or singular institutions are not enough. Instead, government should take a more holistic approach to local government finance system design at a critical juncture in its potential reform, recognising the interconnections and feedback loops in the system. Policy makers need to be flexible and responsive to emerging challenges, rather than relying on rigid and detached solutions.

References

Geissler, R., Hammerschmid, G. & Raffer, C. Eds (2021) Local public finance: An international comparative regulatory perspective. Springer.

Institute for Fiscal Studies. (2023). *How much public spending does each area receive? Local authority level estimates of health, police, school and local government spending*. IFS.

Katz, B., & Bradley, J. (2013). *The metropolitan revolution: How cities and metros are fixing our broken politics and fragile economy*. Brookings Institution Press.

LG Futures. (2017). *Reforming local authority needs assessment*. Communities and Local Government Committee.

Redmond Review. (2020). *Independent review into the oversight of local audit and the transparency of local authority financial reporting*.

Muldoon-Smith, K., & Sandford, M. (2021). Grasping the nettle: The central–local constraints on local government funding in England. *Territory, Politics, Governance, 1-18*. https://doi.org/10.1080/21622671.2021.1924249

9

Conclusion: Redefining the Magic Money Tree

Embedded Autonomy and Resilience

The concept of 'embedded autonomy' overcomes the dualistic contrast between centralism and—as a counter to centralism—aspirations to local government 'autonomy'. Both these perspectives arise from the British Political Tradition (Richards et al., 2024; Marsh & Hall, 2007), for which parliamentary sovereignty embodies a single source of power—the Crown in Parliament. Relationships with other governmental actors are managed through discretion and understandings rather than rules—"an organic approach emphasising order and continuity through incremental adaptation" (Richards et al., 2024, p. 3).

The 2024 Labour government is facing pressure to introduce change into the local government sector. As noted earlier, the sector is struggling with extreme financial stress, few sources of local revenue, and is struggling to provide statutory services. Conversely, much optimism has been invested in the capability of metro-mayors to revitalise local areas and central–local relationships. Large quantities of ideas for reforms have appeared since 2020 (for instance, Hawksbee, 2022; Mudie et al., 2023; Paun et al., 2024; Lucas & Hopkins, 2024), and themes have emerged:

K. Muldoon-Smith et al., *Embedded Autonomy*,
https://doi.org/10.1007/978-981-97-9030-2_9

additional powers, greater control over local revenue, strengthened accountability relationships, improved regulatory relationships.

In such a crowded field, what can the concept of embedded autonomy add? First, it demands a shift in the culture of central–local relations. In doing so, it addresses the question that dogs any reform to UK governance: what happens when the central government does not like something and simply reaches for discretionary powers to stop it? Embedded autonomy implies that decision-making processes, transparency requirements, and financial powers would be defined, at least to some degree, in legislation. In the context of the UK's uncodified constitution, the significance of legislative requirements—which would be justiciable—should not be underestimated. They would provide a foundation and incentive for local government to be regarded with parity of esteem and create a ratchet effect where it is more difficult to retreat from reform than go forward. In Germany the autonomy and finances of local government are founded in the constitution, but in Italy and Japan these system features are defined in ordinary legislation. The UK's uncodified constitution does not preclude effective reforms.

Second, embedded autonomy embodies a vision for different sectors of government to work together, if not always with fully shared purposes. Each tier has its democratic mandate respected. It avoids the zero-sum understanding of autonomy shared by some actors at both central and local levels—for whom "self-sufficient local government" is the ideal endpoint. That perspective reproduces the UK's traditional 'central autonomy' approach. It underlies every complaint from local authorities that their expertise and local relationships are disregarded by central policymakers. By contrast, embedded autonomy emphasises that local authorities and central government are engaged in a joint governance enterprise: developing economies, delivering public services, and assisting their citizens. The Labour government's new Council for the Nations and Regions could provide a starting-point for this type of relationship.

Third, embedded autonomy includes provisions for local authorities to be held accountable transparently by independent authorities. It recognises that, to balance financial discretion, the legality and propriety of decision-making should be open to external examination and assessment/

measurement—but that this cannot become simply a stick for the centre to beat local authorities with. It retains the power for central government to intervene in local authorities that have behaved illegally or hit severe financial difficulties—but to do so in defined circumstances and with a defined role. This is not an easy option for the local authorities: municipalities in Italy and Germany can be and have been forced to significantly increase local taxes to solve a financial crisis, for instance. Equally, authorities in the case study countries are subject to a degree of due diligence when borrowing funds. In contrast, English authorities are ostensibly more liberated in that regard—but curbing that freedom need not lead to a more restrictive system overall.

Why Embedded Autonomy?

Embedded autonomy provides a way to overcome the tension between local government financial autonomy and local government financial resilience. These two principles can be perceived as a trade-off against one another, and even as a point of conflict (Midwinter & Carmichael, 2002). However, learning from the international case studies, the authors argue for a more progressive view of co-dependent autonomy and resilience, with each reinforcing the other in a well-functioning local government finance system. Resilience is an underpinning factor in complex adaptive systems, where disruption is considered inevitable. This provides an alternative to an adversarial pattern of relationships. At the moment, centre and localities comprise opposing sides, often talking past one another.

The centre prioritises control, certainty, stability, and resilience but ignores the political economic reasons why these central aspirations undermine and frustrate local place makers. The local, meanwhile has a more realistic understanding of what is needed in local areas and how solutions could work—but it often loses sight of the pragmatic steps to achieve these solutions, and the legitimate demands of transparency, challenge, and effectiveness. In many ways both sides are often talking about the same thing—certainly they both talk of resilience and the ability to plan but tend to talk past each other from different or slightly oblique perspectives.

Instead, each imperative needs to be balanced and aligned, embedded in an overall system of local government finance where each is a counterbalance for the other. This implies more local sources of finance and more rule-based interactions, establishing parity of esteem for centre and locality: but it also implies enhanced accountability mechanisms, through audit, performance evaluation, and public reporting, particularly around the risk of insolvency. More autonomy and certainty at the local level would allow local authorities to build adaptive capacity to prepare for and respond to budget pressures and shocks to the system. But that capacity is reliant on intergovernmental collaboration, rule-based interactions, developing flexible funding mechanisms, promoting integrated planning, and establishing supportive legislative frameworks. In doing so, it is possible to achieve a balance that maximises the strengths of embedded autonomy and resilience.

The English local government sector may well be hesitant about 'partnership' if that concept does not bring with it a degree of embedded power and parity of esteem. 'Partnership' was an early buzzword of the Blair administrations' stance towards local government: but in time that relationship became characterised by inspections and league tables (Pratchett & Leach, 2003; Jones & Stewart, 2002). That change reflects the historical experience of local government as a second-order policy in the UK, its role and functions driven by UK government spending departments' priorities. The relationship is underpinned by the constant presence of central government discretion towards local authorities (Warner et al., 2024). For instance, the UK's local government legislation contains no requirement for a needs assessment or redistributive funding. It permits central intervention in local authorities for any reason, so long as they can be said to be failing in their 'duty of best value'. There is no legal requirement, or established practice, linking central funding to statutory functions: central funds can be distributed on any basis, and with any conditions, that central government chooses. This extreme absence of rule-based operation is a further feature that distinguishes the English local government finance system from the others outlined in this book.

The Magic Money Tree

There is no magic money tree in English local government—this is because there is no 'new money' in the world of public finance and the pressures on the system of public finance only continue to grow. This situation impacts how local authorities allocate budgets and significantly influence public services, community well-being, and territorial development. We can consider this through the lens of local education and healthcare, transportation, affordable housing, homelessness provision, public safety, parks, cultural venues, and the ability to grant business incentives and invest in urban renewal projects. The ability of local governments to generate and manage financial resources effectively shapes their capacity to invest in infrastructure, provide essential services, and promote economic and social development.

However, it is possible to think differently and consider how the system of local government finance in England can be reformed to tackle the challenges of the present day and the demographic and climate-based challenges coming over the horizon. Returning to the central question in this book—what if local government was funded differently—we have set out how the system of local government finance currently works in England, highlighting the constrains, contradictions, and the inbuilt tension between centralised control and local autonomy. We conclude that existing and proposed sources of income do not address the solvency challenge in English local government—it is likely they do not even come close to doing so. Consequently, utilising the complex system-based perspective, we have examined overseas locations to understand how other countries have grappled with similar situations.

It is important to note that the complex adaptive system perspective in this book does not embody or provoke a silver bullet solution to the problems of local government finance. Instead, it offers an integrated framework for understanding the complications, inefficiencies, and problems in the local government finance system, helping to inform practical strategies and to target finite resource in the most proficient areas. We argue that any reform should view local government finance, and the workings of local government, as a dynamic environment where discretion and flexibility should be built in to enable systems (the overall intergovernmental system) and components of the system (individual local authorities) to change and evolve over time.

It also recognises that for any complex adaptive system to function adequately, in this case the local government finance system, it must have adaptive components and capacity. The components (outlined in Chaps. 5, 6, and 7 and then applied to England in Chap. 8) create capacity in the system (individual local authorities) to evolve over time in response to feedback within the system (spending pressures) and the context outside of the system (new spending imperatives).

Relative needs assessment provides a basis for a meaningful local government finance system that moves beyond unfunded mandates and reconnects spending need with relative resource. There is considerable potential for new research in this area, with the methodologies underpinning such assessment, and their consequences, poorly understood and lacking in transparency (LG Futures, 2017). The meaningful assessment of needs then enables a system of equalisation to manage the variegated nature of local government finance—some locations simply have access to more buoyant local income bases than others, and yet more have differing spending pressures. A clear finding from the overseas research is that any system that has embedded autonomy and system-based resilience also has a well-functioning method for monitoring and managing financial scrutiny—the three-card system in Japan illustrates a legible means of achieving this, significantly reducing indicators of insolvency in recent years. There is considerable opportunity to consider how a similar method could be adopted in England, potentially remodelling existing methods of data capture.

The system of monitoring and scrutiny should be complemented by a standing conference, similar to that seen in Italy that seeks to smooth relations between scales of government and those invested in audit and decision making. It is imperative that this conference complements existing arrangements convened by the existing Local Government Association and those proposed between national government and the expanding combined authority mayoralties. At the time of writing, metro-mayors appear increasingly central to the UK Government's developing policy agenda, but details are still awaited on what additional powers they can anticipate, and associated debates over funds have yet to begin. The role of a standing conference would need to reflect those decisions. It is also important that a standing conference between central and local government is not superseded by the Council of the Nations and Regions,[1] and that it operates separately under its own mandate and independence.

The first five proposals introduced in Chap. 8 indicate how a system of local government finance could better function. However, there is no disguising that the alternative sources of revenue currently being debated are limited. Local charges, tourism taxes, and increased property tax are peripheral in revenue terms and uneven in geographical terms. The actual and potential sources of funding presented in Chap. 4 do not reveal a magic money tree that can be tapped at will to stave off financial struggles. Central government enthusiasm for funding local authorities via the financial benefits of growth has been echoed, throughout the 2010s, in the local government sector's support for greater capacity to raise local revenue in order to drive local growth. This has been repeated by the 2024 Labour government administration. However, the sources of local revenue highlighted—typically business rates—do not generate revenue at the scale required to maintain existing public service levels.

The increasing interest in these sources simply reflects that English local government has exhausted the options available to maintain its portfolio of service provision and community maintenance. An approach akin to the Trinity Reform in Japan would enable English local government to realign its financing through the assignment of major tax resources traditionally held by central government in England, particularly VAT and income tax (the final proposal outlined in Chap. 8). This would strengthen the conditions for local government to have the financial resource to fully consider its place-based objectives. There is considerable potential for further research in this area, understanding how a similar transfer of resource could happen in England, and particularly how this type of change could be cost neutral within the overall government spending envelope.

[1] The multi-tier systems of inter-governmental working in all three case studies portray how a relationship between local authority, combined authority, and state could work.

Japan: Progress in Adversity

During the early 2000s, Japan went through the Trinity Reform and radically reformed their underlying system of local government finance system. This process of change management offers insight into how the legislative change could happen in England and some of the pitfalls to avoid in rapid institutional change, a risk in any critical juncture when change can happen very rapidly (Sorensen, 2023). The Trinity Reform happened in conditions that are almost identical to those witnessed in England today. Japanese government was preoccupied with issues of fiscal soundness, the clear expectation that even more money would be needed in the future to manage the fallout of declining birth rates and an ageing population and a collective consensus around establishing a new local government finance system in which local authorities can make their own decisions.

Ahead of the Trinity Reform, there was a clear discrepancy between the scale of total local government expenditure and total available local revenue, with the balance made up of money transferred from central government with various obligations and ring-fencing arrangements. At the time the comparative scale of national and local government expenditure could be considered on a ratio of 4:6 (Ikawa, 2008). However, the ratio was 6:4 in terms of the redistribution of total tax paid by citizens and businesses—revealing a discrepancy and mismatch between the scale of spending need and the location and control of revenue that contradicted the movement towards decentralisation in Japan. Following legislation, including the Basic Policy on Economic and Fiscal Management and Structural Reform and the Tri-Pillar Reform (agreed in 2005), the principles for rectifying this discrepancy were enacted, with ¥3 trillion to be transferred from national to local government in 2006.

Several key lessons can be taken from the experience in Japan in the early 2000s. While the Trinity Reform can be seen as a broadly successful financial transition, there were significant trade-offs, local discrepancies, and intergovernmental friction because the reform was developed and delivered quickly without considering the inter-relation and impact on the overall local government finance system (Ikawa, 2008; Hirashima,

2020). The Trinity Reform was led by the Ministry of Internal Affairs and Communication (the equivalent of the Ministry of Housing, Communities and Local Government in England). In reflecting on the implementation of the Trinity Reform, the then head of the department, Shogo Hayashi, reflected that the reform was delivered quickly and without always having the full cooperation of the Ministry of Finance (the equivalent of the Treasury in England) and other ministers who held associated budgets.

The reform was also carried out without the full cooperation of local government, with those expected to benefit from the reform being some of the most vociferous critics of the Trinity Reform. This was because the removal of government transfers and the transfer of taxes led to some local authorities being worse off in comparative terms. In England, any transition must also include the collective voice of local government, with government working in tandem with the standing conference proposed in Chap. 8. In addition, to account for any discrepancy between winners and losers in the proposed fiscal realignment, the model of equalisation also proposed in Chap. 8 would adjust for relative loss. There is also a need to avoid the perception in some quarters in Japan that the Trinity Reform, in transferring and assigning so much tax to the local level, removed the incentive to cultivate the local tax base.

Sustaining Change

Echoing the arguments of Pike (2023), the challenge of reconciling local government financial autonomy and resilience arguably begins with normative questions of what local government is for in the first place and how it should then be funded. The findings and recommendations in this book highlight the challenge of not having a codified constitution underpinning the role of local government. The lack of a codified constitution in the UK contributes to the ambiguous and often unclear role of local government. Fixed coordinates and binding points of reference for underpinning reform of the local government finance system do not exist. Unlike many other democratic nations, the UK does not have a single written constitution that explicitly outlines the underlying vision, powers, and responsibilities of local governments. This then leads to central government retaining significant control over local government, undermining local democracy and responsiveness to local needs. Compounding this situation, local government then relies on central government for funding, which is heavily politicised and can be subject to economic fluctuation.

Instead, local government powers and structures are derived from a combination of statutes, common law, and conventions, largely hidden within England's unwritten constitution. The main argument for the approach in England, a constitution that exists but at the same time does not, is that it provides flexibility and discretion in decision making (Lammy, 2020). However, for local government this ambiguity leads to the exact opposite—lack of discretion and uncertainty in the roles and responsibilities of local governments. Responsibilities, between central and local government, overlap without clarity around powers while responsibilities can be interpreted differently, leading to inconsistencies in service delivery between locations. The lack of consistency in the unwritten ways or working is also malleable to the prevalent politics of the day, which in turn makes the job of central government more difficult.

However, it is possible to consider how to achieve the same aims in England without a codified constitution, using conventions, common law, and statutes. In the context of a non-codified constitution, where much legislation establishes vast discretion or reserve powers for central government, legislative provisions can have significant effect. Requiring civil servants, local authorities, and potentially the courts to implement and interpret requirements to operate specific types of needs assessment, or a joint consultative body, could have a galvanising effect on change.

Legislative change would be minimally effective unless accompanied by finance reform. The Japanese experience demonstrates how the foundations for proportionate local government financing can be put in place to underwrite the process of devolution and decentralisation. A similar discrepancy exists in England, with financial resources often not accompanying changes to local functions. One option would be a thorough analysis of total government spend across all the major sectors that fall either directly or indirectly on local government and a related analysis of minimum service requirements for the respective areas of local spend.

The latter would form the fixed coordinates for the former, to understand what is required for each service area before understanding spending requirements. This would then underwrite a more robust local income stack for the local government sector.

An added benefit of such an approach is that it would help make the case for place-based budgeting and take forward some of the learning in the Total Place pilots in the 2000s (Denham & Studdert, 2024), by making sure that spending resource follows its proportionate requirement. The system-based perspective that we proposed will help to understand the inter-relationship with the wider local government finance system—for place-based budgeting to be successful it will need equalisation between location.

The concept of embedded autonomy recognises that any local government finance system must achieve a balance between concerns that can never be entirely reconciled. Local authorities benefit from a degree of autonomous decision-making power, but the optimal system includes criteria for intervention in local authorities that experience difficulties. Similarly, local authorities strengthen their local legitimacy through local taxation, but a national redistribution system prevents economic imbalances between locations from impacting on services available to citizens. We hope to have demonstrated in this book that many different ways of conceptualising the role of local government, and thus the appropriate shape of a local government finance system, are available. This can offer perspectives on how to 'fix' the English system—currently a matter of intense, if low-key, concern—that go beyond the terms of debate as they currently stand.

References

Denham, J., & Studdert, J. (2024). *Place-based public service budgets: Making public money work better for communities*. New Local.

Hawksbee, A. (2022). *Give Back control: Realising the potential of England's mayors*. UK Onward.

Hirashima, H. (2020). A retrospective on the triangle reform of Japan's local government fiscal system. Rikkyo. *Journal of Economics, 74*(1), 121–165.

Ikawa, H. (2008). *Recent local financial system reform (trinity reform)*. COSLOG Up-to-date documents on local autonomy in Japan No.2.
Jones, G., & Stewart, J. (2002). Central-local relations since the Layfield report. *Local Government Studies, 28*(3), 7–28. https://doi.org/10.1080/714004155
LG Futures. (2017). *Reforming local authority needs assessment*. Communities and Local Government Committee.
Lucas, B., & Hopkins, E. (2024). *Impactful devolution 01: A new framework for inclusive growth and national renewal*. Future Governance Forum.
Marsh, D., & Hall, M. (2007). The British political tradition: Explaining the fate of new Labour's constitutional reform agenda. *British Politics, 2*, 215–238. https://doi.org/10.1057/palgrave.bp.4200055
Midwinter, A., & Carmichael, P. (2002). Central Grants and local spending in Britain: A reappraisal of the post-Layfield period. *Local Government Studies, 28*(3), 49–73. https://doi.org/10.1080/714004156
Mudie, R., Singh, T., Fogden, R., Franklin, B., & Geddis, P. (2023). *Funding fair growth: How to transform the UK economy*. Centre for Progressive Policy.
Paun, A., Pope, T., Fright, M., McKee, R., & Allen, B. (2024). *How the next government should complete the job of English devolution*. Institute for Government.
Pike, A. (2023). *Financialization and local statecraft*. Oxford University Press—United Kingdom.
Pratchett, L., & Leach, S. (2003). Local government: Choice within constraint. *Parliamentary Affairs, 57*(2), 366–379. https://doi.org/10.1093/pa/gsh030
Richards, D., Smith, M. J., Warner, S., & Marsh, D. (2024). Crisis what crisis?' Understanding the recurring problems of the British state. *British Journal of Politics and International Relations, 0*(0)—on-line first. https://doi.org/10.1177/13691481241269329.
Sorensen, A. (2023). Urban intensification and land value capture in Toronto: Conjunctural analysis, critical junctures, and developmental pathways in urban planning. *Environment and Planning A: Economy and Space, 0*(0)—Online First. https://doi.org/10.1177/0308518X231216535.
Warner, S., Newman, J., Diamond, P., & Richards, D. (2024). The challenge of devolved English governance and the rise of political spatial inequality. *Parliamentary Affairs, 0*. - on-line first. https://doi.org/10.1093/pa/gsae024

References

Aalbers, M. B. (2015). The potential for financialization. *Dialogues in Human Geography, 5*(2), 214–219. https://doi.org/10.1177/2043820615588158
Akihide, H. (2020). A retrospective on the triangle reform of Japan's local government fiscal system. Rikkyo. *Journal of Economics, 74*(1), 121–165. https://doi.org/10.14992/00020010
Allen, P. M. (2012). Cities: The visible expression of co evolving complexity. In J. Portugali, H. Meyer, E. Stolk, & T. Ekim (Eds.), *Complexity theories of cities have come of age* (pp. 67–89). Springer.
Ambrosanio, M. F., Balduzzi, P., & Bordignon, M. (2016). Economic crisis and fiscal federalism in Italy. In E. Ahmad, M. Ambrosanio, & G. Brosio (Eds.), *Multi-level finance and the euro crisis* (pp. 212–246). Edward Elgar.
Arnold, C. A. (2010). Adaptive watershed planning and climate change. *Environmental and Energy Law and Policy Journal, 5*(2), 417–487.
Banca D'Italia. (2023). *Local government debt: Statistics.*
Bates, D. (2018) *Business rate growth 2017–18.* https://www.linkedin.com/pulse/business-rates-growth-201718-dan-bates/?articleId=6472949282805673984.
Berins Collier, R., & Collier, D. (1991). *Shaping the political arena.* Princeton University Press.
Bessho, S.-I. (2016). *Case study of central and local government finance in Japan.* Asian Development Bank Institute.

K. Muldoon-Smith et al., *Embedded Autonomy*,
https://doi.org/10.1007/978-981-97-9030-2

Beswick, J., & Penny, J. (2018). Demolishing the present to sell off the future? The emergence of 'financialized municipal entrepreneurialism' in London. *International Journal of Urban and Regional Research, 42*(4), 612–632. https://doi.org/10.1111/1468-2427.12612

Beznoska, M., & Kauder, B. (2019). *Debt and investments in municipalities in Germany*. German Economic Institute.

Boettcher, F., Freier, R., Geissler, R., & Niemann, F.-S. (2017). Konsolidierungsprogramme für finanzschwache Kommunen. *Wirtschafsdienst, 8*, 592–599. https://doi.org/10.1007/s10273-018-2336-1

Boggero, G. (2016). The establishment of metropolitan cities in Italy: An advance or a setback for Italian regionalism? *Perspectives on Federalism, 8*(3), 1–22. https://doi.org/10.1515/pof-2016-0014

Bovaird, T. (2008). Emergent strategic management and planning mechanisms in complex adaptive systems: The case of the UK best value initiative. *Public Management Review, 10*(3), 319–340. https://doi.org/10.1080/14719030802002741

Bradbury, J. (2006). *Territory and power* revisited: Theorising territorial politics in the United Kingdom after devolution. *Political Studies, 54*(3), 559–582. https://doi.org/10.1111/j.1467-9248.2006.00615

Branz, J. (2023). *Italy: Regional devolution plan could exacerbate divides, test predictability of public finances*. Scope Ratings. European Rating Agency.

Brosio, G. (2018). Ambition beyond feasibility? Equalization transfers to regional and local governments in Italy. *Budget and Public Expenditure, 92*, 135154.

Brugnano, C., Ferraina, G., Loi, F., Minzyuk, L., & Nitti, M. (2020) *Fiscal federalism and equalisation design under the growing public finance constraint: A case of Italian municipalities*. MPRA Paper 102001, University Library of Munich.

Bucci, V., Ferrara, G., & Resce, G. (2023). Local government spending efficiency and fiscal decentralization: Evidence from Italian municipalities. *Applied Economics, 56*(5), 599–614. https://doi.org/10.1080/00036846.2023.2169241

Bullerjahn, M., & Thöne, J. (2020). *Municipal finance and municipal financial equalisation in Germany*. Deutsche Gesellschaft für Internationale Zusammenarbeit (GIZ) GmbH.

Bulpitt, J. (1983). *Territory and power in the United Kingdom*. Manchester University Press.

Capoccia, G., & Kelemen, R. D. (2007). The study of critical junctures: Theory, narrative, and counterfactuals in historical institutionalism. *World Politics, 59*(3), 341–369. https://doi.org/10.1017/S0043887100020852

Carmichael, P. (1996). The changing territorial operating code of the United Kingdom: Evidence from Northern Ireland. *Public Administration, 74*(3), 413–433. https://doi.org/10.1111/j.1467-9299.1996.tb00878.x

Centre for Cities. (2019). *What does Japan tell us about the potential for fiscal devolution?* Centre for Cities.

Centre for Cities. (2023, June 8). *Potluck: What government needs to do to streamline local government funding.* Centre for Cities Briefing.

Charbit, C. (2020). From "de jure" to "de facto" decentralised public policies: The multi-level governance approach. *The British Journal of Politics and International Relations, 22*(4), 809–819. https://doi.org/10.1177/1369148120937624

Chartered Institute for Public Finance and Accountancy. (2019). *An introductory guide to local government finance.* CIPFA.

Christophers, B. (2018). *The new enclosure: The appropriation of public land in neoliberal Britain.* Verso.

Clark, P., & Rosales, A. (2022). Broadened embedded autonomy and Latin America's pink tide: Towards the neo-developmental state. *Globalizations, 20*(1), 20–37. https://doi.org/10.1080/14747731.2022.2032986

Cochrane, A. (1993). *What ever happened to local government?* Open University Press.

Congress on Local and Regional Authorities. (2017, October 18). *Local and regional democracy in Italy.* Monitoring Committee. Council of Europe.

Constitution of the Italian Republic. (2001). *Published by the parliamentary information, archives and publications office of the senate service for official reports and communication.*

Copus, C., Robert's, M., & Wall, R. (2017). *Local government in England: Centralisation, autonomy and control.* Palgrave Macmillan.

Corte dei Conti. (2019, dicembre 11). *Audizione della Corte dei Conti sui Sistemi Tributari delle Regioni e degli Enti Territoriali nella prospettiva dell'attuazione del Federalismo Fiscale e dell'Autonomia Differenziata, VI COMMISSIONE PERMANENTE FINANZE.*

Council of Local Authorities for International Relations. (2022). *Local government in Japan 2020.* 2022 Revised Edition.

Crivello, S., & Staricco, L. (2017). Institutionalising metropolitan cities in Italy. Success and limits of a centralistic, simplifying approach. *Urban Research & Practice, 10*(2), 228–238. https://doi.org/10.1080/17535069.2017.1307001

de Roo, G. (2007). Shifts in planning practice and theory: From a functional towards a communicative rationale. In G. de Roo & G. Porter (Eds.), *Fuzzy planning: The role of actors in a fuzzy governance environment* (pp. 103–114). Ashgate.

De Siano, R., & D'Uva, M. (2017). Fiscal decentralisation and spillover effects of local government public spending: The case of Italy. *Regional Studies, 51*(10), 1507–1517. https://doi.org/10.1080/00343404.2016.1208814

De Widt, D. (2017). The sustainability of local government finances in England, Germany, and The Netherlands: The impact of intergovernmental regulatory regimes. In M. P. R. Bolivar (Ed.), *Financial sustainability in public administration* (pp. 193–225). Palgrave Macmillan.

Deas, I., Haughton, G., & Ward, K. (2020). Scalar postpolitics, inclusive growth and inclusive economies: Challenging the greater Manchester agglomeration model. *Cambridge Journal of Regions, Economy and Society*. https://doi.org/10.1093/cjres/rsaa022

Demos. (2024). *Liberated public services: A new vision for citizens, professionals and policy makers*. Demos.

Denham, J., & Studdert, J. (2024). *Place-based public service budgets: Making public money work better for communities*. New Local.

Dietz, T., Ostrom, E., & Stern, P. C. (2003). The struggle to govern the commons. *Science, 302*(5652), 1907–1912. https://doi.org/10.1126/science.1091015

DLUHC. (2024a). *Local authority capital expenditure and receipts in England: 2023 to 2024 final outturn*.

DLUHC. (2024b). *Local government financial statistics England no.34 2024*. UK Government.

Eckersley, P. (2024). Financial precarity in English local government. *IPPR Progressive Review, 31*(2), 89–94. https://doi.org/10.1111/newe.12393

Edmiston, D., & Nichols, A. (2018). Social impact bonds: The role of private capital in outcome-based commissioning. *Journal of Social Policy, 47*(1), 57–76. https://doi.org/10.1017/S0047279417000125

Evans, P. (1995). *Embedded autonomy: States and industrial transformation*. Princeton University Press.

Färber, G., & Salm, M. (2015). (De-)centralised social transfers and services in Germany: Between central regulation and efficient local allocation. In J. Kim & N. J. Mau (Eds.), *Decentralisation of education, health and social protection: Issues and challenges*. Published by the Korea Institute of Public Finance and the Danish Ministry for Economic Affairs and the Interior.

Ferry, L. (2019). *Audit and inspection of local authorities in England: Five years after the local audit and accountability act 2014*. Communities and Local Government Committee.

Ferry, L., & Eckersley, P. (2020). Hybridizing the institutional logics of performance improvement and budgetary stewardship in English and welsh local government. *Public Policy and Administration, 35*(1), 45–64. https://doi.org/10.1177/0952076718781433

Ferry, L., Eckersley, P., & Zakaria, Z. (2015). Accountability and transparency in English local government: Moving from matching parts to awkward couple? *Financial Accountability and Management, 31*(3), 345–361. https://doi.org/10.1111/faam.12060

Fields, D. (2018). Constructing a new asset class: Property-led financial accumulation after the crisis. *Economic Geography, 94*(2), 118–140. https://doi.org/10.1080/00130095.2017.1397492

Foster, C. D., Jackman, R., & Perlman, M. (1980). *Local government finance in a unitary state*. George Allen and Unwin.

Fraser, A., Tan, S., Lagarde, M., & Mays, N. (2018). Narratives of promise, narratives of caution: A review of the literature on social impact bonds. *Social Policy and Administration, 52*(1), 4–28. https://doi.org/10.1111/spol.12260

French, M., Hesselgreaves, H., Wilson, R., Hawkins, M., & Lowe, T. (2023). *Harnessing complexity for better outcomes in public and not-for-profit services*. Bristol University Press.

Fuller, C. (2018). Entrepreneurial urbanism, austerity and economic governance. *Cambridge Journal of Regions, Economy and Society, 11*(3), 565–585. https://doi.org/10.1093/cjres/rsy023

Gagliano, A. (2013). The introduction of the 'balanced budget' principle into the Italian constitution: What perspectives for the financial autonomy of regional and local governments? *Perspectives on Federalism, 5*(1), 79–96. https://ssrn.com/abstract=2421383

Geissler, R. (2020). Germany report. In R. Geissler, G. Hammerschmid, & C. Raffer (Eds.), *Local public finance in Europe: Country reports*. Bertelsmann Stiftung and Hertie School of Governance.

Geissler, R., Hammerschmid, G. & Raffer, C. Eds (2021) Local public finance: An international comparative regulatory perspective. Springer.

Geyer, R., & Cairney, P. (2015). *Handbook on complexity and public policy*. Edward Elgar.

Geyer, R., & Rihani, S. (2010). *Complexity and public policy: A new approach to 21st Century politics, policy and society*. Routledge.

Gray, M., & Barford, A. (2018). The depths of the cuts: The uneven geography of local government austerity. *Cambridge Journal of Regions, Economy and Society, 11*(3), 541–563. https://doi.org/10.1093/cjres/rsy019

Greenhalgh, P., Muldoon-Smith, K., Adebayo, A., & Ellis, J. (2018, June 27–30) Experimental spatial modelling of commercial property stock using GIS. In *European real estate research society conference*, Reading.

Greenhalgh, P., Muldoon-Smith, K., & Angus, S. (2016). Commercial property tax in the UK: Business rates and rating appeals. *Journal of Property Investment and Finance, 34*(6), 602–619. https://doi.org/10.1108/JPIF-03-2016-0014

Haasnoot, M., Kwakkel, J. H., Walker, W. E., & ter Maat, J. (2013). Dynamic adaptive policy pathways: A method for crafting robust decisions for a deeply uncertain world. *Global Environmental Change, 23*(2), 485–498. https://doi.org/10.1016/j.gloenvcha.2012.12.006

Hall, P. A. (2016). Politics as a process structured in space and time. In K. O. Fioretos, T. G. Falleti, & A. D. Sheingate (Eds.), *The Oxford handbook of historical institutionalism* (pp. 31–50). Oxford University Press.

Hall, S. (2011). The neo-liberal revolution. *Cultural Studies, 25*(6), 705–728. https://doi.org/10.1080/09502386.2011.619886

Hasenberger, H. (2024). What is local government financialisation? Four empirical channels to clarify the roles of local government. *Urban Studies, 61*(11), 2039–2059. https://doi.org/10.1177/00420980231222133

Hastings, A., Bailey, N., & Gannon., K. Besemer., & G. Bramley. (2015). Coping with the cuts? The Management of the Worst Financial Settlement in living memory. *Local Government Studies, 41*(4), 601–621. https://doi.org/10.1080/03003930.2015.1036987

Hawksbee, A. (2022). *Give Back control: Realising the potential of England's mayors*. UK Onward.

Heinelt, H., & Stolzenberg, P. (2014). 'The Rhinish Greeks'. Bailout funds for local government in German federal states. *Urban Research & Practice, 7*, 228–240. https://doi.org/10.1080/17535069.2014.910934

Hirota, H., & Yunoue, H. (2022). Fiscal rules and creative accounting: Evidence from Japanese municipalities. *Journal of the Japanese and International Economies, 63*, 101172. https://doi.org/10.1016/j.jjie.2021.101172

Holland, J. (2024) *Governments use of exceptional financial support at best careless and maybe reckless*. Room151. Retrieved June 13, 2024, from https://www.room151.co.uk/funding/exceptional-financial-support-careless-reckless/

Hood, C. (2010). Accountability and transparency: Siamese twins, matching parts, awkward couple? *West European Politics, 33*(5), 989–1009. https://doi.org/10.1080/01402382.2010.486122

Hutton, W. (2024, February 4). *The Tories starved councils, thinking no one cared. Now they're bust—And we care very much.* The Observer.

Ikawa, H. (2008). *Recent local financial system reform (trinity reform).* COSLOG Up-to-date documents on local autonomy in Japan No.2.

Insol International. (2022). *When liquidation is not an option: A global study on the treatment of public entities in distress.* Insol International.

Institute for Fiscal Studies. (2019). *Taking control: Which taxes could be devolved to local government?* IFS.

Institute for Fiscal Studies. (2023). *How much public spending does each area receive? Local authority level estimates of health, police, school and local government spending.* IFS.

Institute for Fiscal Studies. (2024). *How have English councils' funding and spending changed? 2010 to 2024.* IFS.

Institute for Government. (2020). *Local government funding in England.* Institute for Government.

Institute for Government. (2023). *How can devolution deliver regional growth in England.* Institute for Government.

Jacobs, A. J. (2003). Embedded autonomy and uneven metropolitan development: A comparison of the Detroit and Nagoya auto regions, 1969-2000. *Urban Studies, 40*(2), 335–360. https://doi.org/10.1080/00420980220080301

Japan Finance Organisation for Local Authorities. (2022). *Annual Report.* JFM.

Japanese Ministry of Finance. (2023). *White paper on local government finance: Fact sheet.* Japanese Government.

Jones, G., & Stewart, J. (2002). Central-local relations since the Layfield report. *Local Government Studies, 28*(3), 7–28. https://doi.org/10.1080/714004155

Kameda, T., Namba, R., & Tsuruga, T. (2021). Decomposing local fiscal multipliers: Evidence from Japan. *Japan and the World Economy, 57*, 101053. https://doi.org/10.1016/j.japwor.2021.101053

Kato, S., & Ahern, J. (2008). Learning by doing: Adaptive planning as a strategy to address uncertainty in planning. *Journal of Environmental Planning and Management, 51*(4), 543–559. https://doi.org/10.1080/09640560802117028

Katz, B., & Bradley, J. (2013). *The metropolitan revolution: How cities and metros are fixing our broken politics and fragile economy.* Brookings Institution Press.

Keith-Lucas, B., & Richards, P. G. (1978). *A history of local government in the twentieth century.* Routledge.

Kim, Y., & Warner, M. (2020). Pragmatic municipalism or austerity urbanism? Understanding local government responses to fiscal stress. *Local Government Studies*. https://doi.org/10.1080/03003930.2020.1729751

Kimura, S. (2015). Goals and reforms of the current Japanese local tax system. *Hitotsubashi Journal of Law and Politics, 43*, 17–48.

Klijn, E. H. (2008). Complexity theory and public administration: What's new? Key concepts in complexity theory compared to their counterparts in public administration research. *Public Management Review, 10*(3), 299–317. https://doi.org/10.1080/14719030802002675

Lennkh-Yunus, Y. (2023). *Italian Republic rating report*. Scope Ratings for the Sovereign and Public Sector.

Levelling Up, Housing and Communities Committee. (2024). *Financial distress in local authorities—Financial distress in local authorities enquiry report*. HM Government.

LG Futures. (2017). *Reforming local authority needs assessment*. Communities and Local Government Committee.

Lin, G. C. S., Smart, A., Li, X., & Hu, F. Z. Y. (2019). Financializing Chinese cities: State–capital nexus and the uneven geography of housing speculation. *Area Development and Policy, 4*(4), 435–453. https://doi.org/10.1080/23792949.2019.1625277

Local Government Association. (2022). *Reforming revenues: Options for the future financing of local government*. LGA.

Local Government Association. (2024). *Local government white paper*. LGA.

Local Government Information Unit. (2024). *The state of local government finance*. LGIU.

Lowe, T., French, M., Hawkins, M., Hesselgreaves, H., & Wilson, R. (2021). New development: Responding to complexity in public services—the human learning systems approach. *Public Money & Management, 41*(7), 573–576. https://doi.org/10.1080/09540962.2020.1832738

Lowndes, V., & Gardner, A. (2016). Local governance under the conservatives: Super-austerity, devolution and the 'smarter state'. *Local Government Studies, 42*(3), 357–375. https://doi.org/10.1080/03003930.2016.1150837

Lowndes, V., & McCaughie, K. (2013). Weathering the perfect storm? Austerity and institutional resilience in local government. *Politics & Policy, 41*(4), 533–549. https://doi.org/10.1332/030557312X655747

Lucas, B., & Hopkins, E. (2024). *Impactful devolution 01: A new framework for inclusive growth and national renewal*. Future Governance Forum.

Machidori, S. (2023). *Decentralisation reforms, in: Political reform reconsidered: The trajectory of a transformed Japanese state*. Springer.

MacKinnon, D. (2015). Devolution, state restructuring and policy divergence in the UK. *The Geographical Journal, 181*(1), 47–56. https://doi.org/10.1111/geoj.12057

Mahoney, J. (2000) Path dependence in historical sociology. *Theory and Society, 29*(4), 507–548. https://www.jstor.org/stable/3108585

Marsh, D., & Hall, M. (2007). The British political tradition: Explaining the fate of new Labour's constitutional reform agenda. *British Politics, 2*, 215–238. https://doi.org/10.1057/palgrave.bp.4200055

Marsh, D., Richards, D., & Smith, M. (2003). Unequal plurality: Towards an asymmetric power model of British politics. *Government and Opposition, 38*(3), 306–322. https://doi.org/10.1111/1477-7053.t01-1-00017

Mertens, A., Trampusch, C., Fastenrath, F., & Wangemann, R. (2019). The political economy of local government financialization and the role of policy diffusion. *Regulation and Governance*. https://doi.org/10.1111/rego.12285

MHCLG. (2017). *A new approach to developer contributions*. UK Government.

Midwinter, A., & Carmichael, P. (2002). Central Grants and local spending in Britain: A reappraisal of the post-Layfield period. *Local Government Studies, 28*(3), 49–73. https://doi.org/10.1080/714004156

Ministry of Internal Affairs and Communication. (2022). *Japanese local government white paper*.

Ministry of the Interior. (2022a). *The investments of local authorities: Trend analysis and actions per ilrilancio*. Ministry of the Interior.

Ministry of the Interior. (2022b). *Financial critical issues of local authorities: Causes and points of reflection for a reform of prevention and remediation procedures*. Observatory on the Finance and Accounting of Local Authorities—Rome.

Mor, F., & Sandford, M. (2017). Growing pains: Property taxation and revenue incentives in English local government. *Local Economy, 32*(5), 399–419. https://doi.org/10.1177/0269094217720738

Mudie, R., Singh, T., Fogden, R., Franklin, B., & Geddis, P. (2023). *Funding fair growth: How to transform the UK economy*. Centre for Progressive Policy.

Muldoon-Smith, K., & Greenhalgh, P. (2015). Passing the buck without the bucks: Some reflections on fiscal decentralisation and the business rate retention scheme in England. *Local Economy, 30*(6), 609–626. https://doi.org/10.1177/0269094215599724

Muldoon-Smith, K., & Sandford, M. (2021). Grasping the nettle: The central–local constraints on local government funding in England. *Territory, Politics, Governance, 1-18*. https://doi.org/10.1080/21622671.2021.1924249

Murphy, P., Ferry, L., Glennon, R., & Greenhalgh, K. (2019). *Public service accountability: Rekindling a debate*. United Kingdom.

Musgrave, R. (1959). *The theory of public finance*. McGraw-Hill.

National Audit Office. (2020). *Local authority investment in commercial property*. National Audit Office.

National Audit Office. (2021). *The local government finance system in England: Overview and challenges*. National Audit Office.

Newton, K., & Karen, T. J. (1985). *The politics of local expenditure*. Macmillan.

Oates, W. (1972). *Fiscal federalism*. Edward Elgar.

OECD. (2019). *Making decentralisation work handbook for policy makers*. OECD.

OECD. (2022a). *World observatory on subnational government finance and investment—Germany*. Retrieved 23, June 2023, from https://www.sng-wofi.org/country-profiles/

OECD. (2022b). *World observatory on subnational government finance and investment—Italy*. Retrieved 23, June 2023, from https://www.sng-wofi.org/country-profiles/

OECD. (2022c). *World observatory on subnational government finance and investment—Japan*. Retrieved 23, June 2023, from https://www.sng-wofi.org/country-profiles/

OpenCivitas. (2022). *The allocation of the municipal solidarity fund*. OpenCivitas—Ministry of Local Government Finance.

Padovani, E., Rescigno, L., & Ceccatelli, J. (2018). Municipal bond debt and sustainability in a non-mature financial market: The case of Italy. *Sustainability, 10*, 1–25. https://doi.org/10.3390/su10093249

Patterson, T. M., Niccolucci, V., & Marchettini, N. (2008). Adaptive environmental management of tourism in the province of Siena, Italy using the ecological footprint. *Journal of Environmental Management, 86*(2), 407–418. https://doi.org/10.1016/j.jenvman.2006.04.017

Paun, A., Pope, T., Fright, M., McKee, R., & Allen, B. (2024). *How the next government should complete the job of English devolution*. Institute for Government.

Peck, J. (2010). *Constructions of neoliberal reason*. University Press.

Peck, J. (2017a). Transatlantic city, part 1: Conjunctural urbanism. *Urban Studies, 54*(1), 4–30. https://doi.org/10.1177/0042098016679355

Peck, J. (2017b). Transatlantic city, part 2: Late entrepreneurialism. *Urban Studies, 54*(2), 327–363. https://doi.org/10.1177/0042098016683859

Peck, J., & Tickell, A. (2002). A neoliberalizing space. *Antipode, 34*(3), 380–404. https://doi.org/10.1111/1467-8330.00247

Peck, J., & Whiteside, H. (2016). Financializing Detroit. *Economic Geography, 92*(3), 235–268. https://doi.org/10.1080/00130095.2015.1116369

Penny, J. (2022). Revenue generating machines? London's local housing companies and the emergence of the local state rentierism. *Antipode, 54*(2), 545–566. https://doi.org/10.1111/anti.12774

Pike, A. (2023). *Financialization and local statecraft*. Oxford University Press—United Kingdom.

Pike, A., O'Brien, P., Strickland, T., & Tomaney, J. (2019a). *Financialising city statecraft and infrastructure*. Edward Elgar.

Pike, A., O'Brien, P., Strickland, T., & Tomaney, J. (2019b). Financialising city statecraft and infrastructure; book symposium. *Environment and Planning A, 52*(4), 790–813. https://doi.org/10.1177/0308518X19889058

Pratchett, L., & Leach, S. (2003). Local government: Choice within constraint. *Parliamentary Affairs, 57*(2), 366–379. https://doi.org/10.1093/pa/gsh030

Preiser, R. (2018). *Key features of complex adaptive systems: And practical implications for guiding action*. CST Policy Brief 2018.

Raffer, C., & Padovani, E. (2020). Italy report. In R. Geissler, G. Hammerschmid, & C. Raffer (Eds.), *Local public finance in Europe: Country reports*. Bertelsmann Stiftung and Hertie School of Governance.

Redmond Review. (2020). *Independent review into the oversight of local audit and the transparency of local authority financial reporting*.

Reuters. (2023). *Borrowing to drive Japan's debt over 1,100 trillion yen for first time*.

Rhodes, M. L., & MacKechnie, G. (2003). Understanding public service systems: Is there a role for complex adaptive systems theory? *Emergence, 5*(4), 57–85. https://doi.org/10.1207/s15327000em0504_6

Richards, D., Smith, M. J., Warner, S., & Marsh, D. (2024). 'Crisis what crisis?' Understanding the recurring problems of the British state. *British Journal of Politics and International Relations, 0*(0)—on-line first. https://doi.org/10.1177/13691481241269329

Rietzler, K., & Truger, A. (2019). Is the "debt brake" behind Germany's successful fiscal consolidation? A comparative analysis of the "structural" consolidation of the government sub-sector budgets from 1991 to 2017. *Dans Revue de l'OFCE, 2*, 11–30.

Rodríguez-Pose, A., & Gill, N. (2003). The global trend towards devolution and its implications. *Environment and Planning C: Government and Policy, 21*(3), 333–351. https://doi.org/10.1068/c0235

Rodríguez-Pose, A., & Vidal-Bover, M. (2022). Unfunded mandates and the economic impact of decentralisation. When finance does not follow function. *Political Studies, 72*(2), 652–676. https://doi.org/10.1177/00323217221136666

Roesel, F. (2017). The political economy of fiscal supervision and budget deficits—Evidence from Germany. *Fiscal Studies, 4*, 641–666. https://www.jstor.org/stable/26605639

Sandford, M. (2016). Public services and local government: The end of the principle of funding following duties. *Local Government Studies, 42*(4), 637–656. https://doi.org/10.1080/03003930.2016.1171753

Sandford, M. (2020) *Local government: Commercial property investments.* Research Briefing. House of Commons Library.

Sandford, M. (2022). *Local government in England: Structures.* House of Commons Library.

Seaton, P. (2010). Depopulation and financial collapse in Yabari: Market forces, administrative folly, or a warning to others? *Social Science Japan Journal, 13*(2), 227–240. https://doi.org/10.1093/ssjj/jyp045

Sengupta, U., Rauws, S. W., & de Roo, G. (2016). Planning and complexity: Engaging with temporal dynamics, uncertainty and complex adaptive systems. *Environment and Planning B: Planning and Design, 43*(6), 970–974. https://doi.org/10.1177/0265813516675872

Skrimizea, E., Haniotou, H., & Parra, C. (2018). On the "complexity turn" in planning: An adaptive rationale to navigate spaces and times of uncertainty. *Planning Theory, 18*(1), 122–142. https://doi.org/10.1177/1473095218780515

Smith, P. (2007). *Formula funding of public services.* Routledge.

Soifer, H. D. (2012). The causal logic of critical junctures. *Comparative Political Studies, 45*(12), 1572–1597. https://doi.org/10.1177/0010414012463902

Sorensen, A. (2023). Urban intensification and land value capture in Toronto: Conjunctural analysis, critical junctures, and developmental pathways in urban planning. *Environment and Planning A: Economy and Space, 0*(0)—Online First. https://doi.org/10.1177/0308518X231216535.

Sotarauta, M. (2016). *Leadership and the city: Power, strategy and networks in the making of knowledge cities.* Routledge.

Spahn, P. B. (2016). Multi-level finance and the euro crisis. The German experience. In E. Ahmad, M. Bordignon, & G. Brosio (Eds.), *Multi-level finance and the euro crisis* (pp. 83–102). Edward Elgar Publishing.

Stevens, A. (2013, July 31). *Japanese city's financial collapse offers a number of interesting lessons.*

Styhre, A. (2019). *The institutional theory of the firm: Embedded autonomy.* Routledge.

Suwalski, J., & Branz, G. (2019). *Italian regions' autonomy plans weigh on the fiscal framework's predictability.* Scope: Scope Ratings.

Tapp, R., & Kay, K. (2019). Fiscal geographies: "Placing" taxation in urban geography. *Urban Geography, 40*(4), 573–581. https://doi.org/10.1080/02723638.2019.1585141

Tiebout, C. (1956). A pure theory of local expenditures. *Journal of Political Economy, 64*(5), 416–424. https://doi.org/10.1086/257839

Travers, T., & Esposito, L. (2004). *Nothing to lose but your chains: Reforming the English local government finance system.* Policy Exchange.

Unlock Democracy. (2021). *Local government in England: Forty years of decline.* Unlock Democracy.

van Buuren, A., Driessen, P. P. J., Rijswick, M. V., Rietveld, P., Salet, W., Spit, T., & Teisman, G. (2013). Towards adaptive spatial planning for climate change: Balancing between robustness and flexibility. *Journal for European Environmental & Planning Law, 10*(1), 29–53. https://doi.org/10.1163/18760104-01001003.

Vines, E. (2014). Reframing *English nationalism and Euroscepticism*: From populism to the British political tradition. *British Politics, 9*(3), 255–274. https://doi.org/10.1057/bp.2014.3

Ward, W., Brill, F., Deruytter, L., & Pike, A. (2024). Local state financialisation: Future research directions for an emergent conjuncture. *Finance and Space, 1*(1), 318–339. https://doi.org/10.1080/2833115X.2024.2380004

Warner, S., Newman, J., Diamond, P., & Richards, D. (2024). The challenge of devolved English governance and the rise of political spatial inequality. *Parliamentary Affairs, 0.* - on-line first. https://doi.org/10.1093/pa/gsae024

Webb, C. (2024. March 11). *Exceptional financial support is general election holding strategy.* Local Government Chronicle.

Weber, R. (2010). Selling city futures: The financialisation of urban redevelopment policy. *Economic Geography, 86*(3), 251–274. https://doi.org/10.1111/j.1944-8287.2010.01077.x

Werner, J. (2018). *Equalisation among the states in Germany: The junction between solidarity and subsidiarity.* Feda.

Westley, F. (2002). The devil in the dynamics: Adaptive management on the front lines. In L. Gunderson & C. S. Holling (Eds.), *Panarchy: Understanding transformations in human and natural systems* (pp. 333–360). Island Press.

Wilson, D., & Game, C. (2011). *Local government in the United Kingdom* (5th ed.). Palgrave Macmillan.

Zabler, S. (2020). Austerity regimes at the local level: Examining fiscal effects of austerity commissioners using a time-series synthetic control method. *Public Performance & Management Review, 43*(2), 414–432. https://doi.org/10.1080/15309576.2019.1676276

Zabler, S. (2021). New ways of limiting local government debt: An empirical assessment of the German case. In T. Bergström, S. Kuhlmann, J. Franzke, & E. Wayenberg (Eds.), *The future of local self-government. Palgrave studies in sub-National Governance* (pp. 243–256).

Zabler, S. (2022). Uncovering the effect of local government debt brakes in Germany using synthetic controls. *Local Government Studies, 48*(5), 864–886. https://doi.org/10.1080/03003930.2021.1986392

Zellner, M., & Campbell, S. D. (2015). Planning for deep-rooted problems: What can we learn from aligning complex systems and wicked problems? *Planning Theory & Practice, 16*(4), 457–478. https://doi.org/10.1080/14649357.2015.1084360

The manufacturer's authorised representative in the EU is Springer Nature Customer Service Centre GmbH, Europaplatz 3, 69115 Heidelberg, Germany. If you have any concerns regarding our products, please contact ProductSafety@springernature.com

Printed and bound by CPI Group (UK) Ltd, Croydon, CR0 4YY
30/09/2026
02225286-0003